10 Simple Habits That Lead to an Organized, Decluttered, and Efficient Home

*Master Your Clutter
and Live a Life of Freedom*

© Copyright 2022 All rights reserved.

Without the prior written permission of the publisher, no part of this publication may be stored in a retrieval system, replicated, or transferred in any form or medium, digital, scanning, recording, printing, mechanical, or otherwise, except as permitted under the 1976 United States Copyright Act, sections 107 and 108. Permission concerns should be directed to the publisher's permission department.

Legal Notice

This book is copyright protected. It is only to be used for personal purposes. Without the author's or publisher's permission, you cannot paraphrase, quote, copy, distribute, sell, or change any part of the information in this book.

Disclaimer

This book is written and published independently. Please keep in mind that the material in this publication is solely for educational and entertainment purposes. All efforts have been made to provide authentic, up-to-date, trustworthy, and comprehensive information. There are no express or implied assurances. The purpose of this book's material is to assist readers in having a better understanding of the subject matter. The activities, information, and exercises are provided solely for self-help information. This book is not intended to replace expert psychological, legal, financial, or other guidance. If you require counseling, please get in touch with a qualified professional.

By reading this text, the reader accepts that the author will not be held liable for any damages, indirectly or directly experienced due to the use of the information included herein, particularly, but not limited to, omissions, errors, or inaccuracies. As a reader, you are accountable for your decisions, actions, and consequences.

TABLE OF CONTENTS

PQ Unleashed Introduction

Introduction

Habit 1: Making Your Home a Priority

  An Organized Home Is a Healthier, Safer Environment

    A Messy Home Can Hinder Your Career

    Clutter Can Affect Your Mental Health

    Being Organized Is More Convenient

  Can Save You Money

  Sets a Good Example

    Greater Love for Your Home

    Cleanliness Is Contagious

    Your Self-Esteem Boost

  Signs That Your Home Is an Unhealthy Place to Live

  Making Your Home a Priority

  How to Convince Members of Your Household to Join Your Journey

  How to Get Your Family to Stay Organized

    Create Designated Spaces

    Create a Visual Weekly Schedule

    Set Up for Success

    Cleaning Routine

    Prioritize What Is Important for Your Family

  How to Keep an Organized House With Roommates

- Key Principles to Consider
- Thoughts for Reflection
- Habit 2: Create a System Around Your Home That Works for You
  - What Exactly Is Home Management?
  - Steps to Start Organizing Your Home
    - Start by Creating a List
    - Adopting a Routine
    - Morning and Evening Routines
    - Weekly Cleaning Routines
    - Adding a Deep Cleaning Routine
  - Installing House Management Systems
  - House Management Checklists
  - Building a Binder
  - How to Make a Binder for Home Management
    - Step 1: Gather Everything You Need
    - Step 2: Making Use of Home Contents in a Binder
    - What Should Be in a Home Management Binder?
    - Step 3: Have a Nice Cover Page
    - Step 4: Adding the Plastic Files
    - Step 5: Add All the Planner Pages in the Right Places in the Binder
    - Step 6: Remember to Fill in the Necessary Information About You on the Pages
  - How to Start With Home Management Systems
    - Start With the Areas Causing the Most Trouble

- Remember to Take It One Step at a Time
- The Secret to Creating a Routine
  - Small Tips for a Good Morning Routine
- How to Implement a Deep Cleaning Routine
- What Are Some Tools to Help With Deep Cleaning?
- Key Principles to Consider
- Thoughts for Reflection
- Habit 3: Keeping Things in the Home Simple
  - Prioritize Your Time
  - How to Avoid Overscheduling
    - Buffer Zones
    - Understand That You Have Limits!
    - Make Use of Technology
    - Do NOT Multitask
    - Allow Yourself to Prioritize the Moment
    - If You Need to "Squeeze" It Into Your Schedule, Just Say No
    - Schedule Some "Me" Time
  - Other Steps to Simplify Your Daily Routines
  - Key Principles to Consider
  - Thoughts for Reflection
- Habit 4: Using Less Stuff and Utilizing More Space
  - Take a Look at Wall Space
  - Double Duty Is Becoming More Popular
  - Awkward Spaces
  - Using Doors

Consider Investing in a Vintage Ladder
Clever Ways to Best Make Use of the Space You Have
Understanding Home Aesthetics
The Importance of Design in the Home Aesthetic
What Is Modern and What is Traditional?
Color Scheme
Space and Areas You Want to Use
Furniture Aesthetics
Aesthetics
Key Principles to Consider
Thoughts for Reflection
Habit 5: Following the One-Minute Rule
Why Is Procrastination So Harmful?
Common Traits of a Procrastinator
Why Do People Procrastinate?
How Do People Procrastinate?
How Do You Overcome Procrastination?
One-Minute Rule
Why Does the One-Minute Rule Work?
Overcoming Chronic Procrastination
Key Principles to Consider
Thoughts for Reflection
Habit 6: Designate a Place for Everything in Your Home
Place the Like Things With the Like Things

Taking an Inventory
Check Out Your Space Before You Start Organizing
Put a Label on Everything
Tackle One Space at a Time
Set Aside Time for Each Project
Key Principles to Consider
Thoughts for Reflection
Habit 7: Place Items in Your Home Where They Will BeUsed Accordingly
Ways to Store at Home
Kitchen Storage
Bathroom Storage
Storage Rules to Follow
Storage Rules for Small Spaces
Key Principles to Consider
Thoughts for Reflection
Habit 8: Avoid Creating Clutter-Collecting Areas
Problem 1
Problem 2
Problem 3
Problem 4
More Tips for Avoiding Clutter
Tricks for Staying More Organized
Top Cleaning Tips
Key Principles to Consider
Thoughts for Reflection

Habit 9: CLAYGO: Clearing Visual Clutter
Differences Between Clutter and Hoarding
What Is Hoarding Exactly?
What Can Hoarding Do?
Dealing With Visual Clutter
What Are the Benefits of Clearing Visual Clutter?
Key Principles to Consider
Thoughts for Reflection
Habit 10: Labeling
Why Is Labeling Important?
Labeling Items in Your Home
The Shared Areas
Key Principles to Consider
Thoughts for Reflection
Conclusion

PQ UNLEASHED INTRODUCTION

"You never touch your true potential until you challenge yourself to go beyond imposed limitations."

Roy T. Bennett

What distinguishes the average from the excellent? It's the ability to unleash the potential which lies within.

Most dictionaries define potential as the "possibility of something developing" or "something that can develop and become actual." This means that it isn't a given or automatic. Everyone has untapped potential, but potential can't grow into anything more if it isn't unleashed into action. This is what the Potential Quotient Unleashed program is here to do.

The Potential Quotient Unleashed (PQ Unleashed) program catalyzes the activation of one's potential by producing well-written books founded on research. These books aim to help readers bring out the possibilities stored within them, even and especially in specific challenging areas. Unlike other self-help books,

PQ Unleashed acknowledges that one's Potential Quotient isn't fixed. It can be developed, appraised, and improved over time. Self-reflective questions are added throughout each chapter to help the reader apply various learnings, not merely based on superficial head knowledge, but through a deeper understanding of the topics' concepts.

Get ready to flourish as your potential turns into true influence and ability!

INTRODUCTION

> Habits change into character. –Ovid

Being a night owl means you live the life of an alien in a world built for mornings and sunlight. I used to be a morning person. Got up each morning, gulped down my cup of coffee, gathered my stuff, and drove to work. Then, after a long, hard day, I would come home, cook up a lazy meal, and while away the rest of my evening doing little bits of nothing. Although I did not do a lot in my home, the state of my home seemed to slowly crumble into chaos.

As time went on, even as my job changed, my habits did not. This meant that, despite having more free time and less work, I still managed to be late yet somehow never managed to wash the dishes.

As it would turn out, time was never a problem later in my life. Time did not dictate my success. The ticking clock did not snatch extra seconds away from me. My own bad habits did the job perfectly well on their own, especially when it came to the condition of my home.

I would complain all the same: I did not have enough time; I was too busy; I am a master procrastinator; I am not a morning person anymore. What I did not realize was these habits were slowly jeopardizing my livelihood, my relationships, and my future. Delaying my home responsibilities until they were urgent led to bouts of great stress and panic. Flurrying like a lost rabbit in a maze, I soon realized things needed to change. With nothing to lose, I took up a pen and wrote down all the goals I wanted to achieve. I then set up a to-do list of what I needed to do to achieve them each and every day. I smiled. I had a plan. I had my goals for my home.

I still failed. My reminders of due dates were piling up alongside the laundry, and I struggled with the same old problems. Why? Because I failed to address the one aspect in my life that was holding me back: habits. Specifically, bad habits that were wrapped around me like weeds stick to soil, and instead of pulling them out by the roots, I was practically watering them.

In the constant cycle of repeating my mistakes, I realized something else needed to change. It didn't just matter what my motivation was because motivation works a lot like a candle:

one blow of procrastination could snuff out the flame—or worse yet, knock the candle over, setting alight all my commitment to maintaining my home.

Rather, it depended on the smaller aspects of my life: habits. Little things that I would do—or not do—each and every day to make sure the necessary tasks got done. I was in the habit of checking my phone and squandering an hour of my time on social media. I was in the habit of starting a task only to turn my attention to the latest quiz on Google. Instead of folding the laundry or emptying the trash, I had far more fun bingeing my newest Netflix addiction.

I would always make up an excuse, but the most common ones were, "Just another five minutes" or "I will do it AFTER I finish with XYZ." Obviously, I was lying to myself as I just slapped the same excuse on the next activity.

Does this sound familiar to you? Do you struggle with procrastination? Are you overwhelmed with completing the right tasks at the right times? Or do you simply want to make some changes to improve your quality of life? It all comes down to one key factor:

Habits.

Habits are the actions a person repeats regularly, usually at the same intervals. They become an ingrained part of our lives. Habits are hard to form and even harder to break.

So in order to boost your quality of life, you want to focus on breaking bad habits that are standing in the way of your growth and success and begin building good habits that encourage and spur progress toward your goals.

This is exactly what I had in mind as I started focusing on my habits: Altering the day-to-day activities and placing a deliberate mental effort on removing the bad habits and adding new, more positive ones. I still find myself faltering from time to time. It has been a journey, one which I intend to share.

Specifically, I want to share 10 habits, which you will find in the 10 chapters, that you can incorporate into your life to help you achieve an organized, decluttered, and efficient home, thereby creating a sense of freedom in your life and in your space. The positive impacts of an efficient home will spill out into various other aspects of your life.

HABIT 1: MAKING YOUR HOME A PRIORITY

Imagine you are working every single day. You get tired as the work never seems to end. You return home with some hopes of relaxing, but as you open the door, you are met with chaos. Papers are strewn across the dining table, dishes are piled in the sink, and a small avalanche of clothing is tumbling out of the closet. You spend a good 15 minutes looking for the spatula in order to cook yourself some dinner. You decide to eat out of the pan because there are no more clean plates. Having spent your evening battling the chaos of your surroundings, you go to bed even more exhausted, wake up, put on some hopefully clean trousers, and soon find yourself heading off to work.

And now the big question: How close is this scenario to your reality?

Now picture this: You work long and hard but have a steady schedule to make sure you get everything done. You return home, place your shoes in their designated spot, and go make dinner. As the food is cooking, you spend an extra five minutes sweeping the living room and wiping the bathroom, all according to plan. You finish up, eat dinner, clean the four dishes you used to cook and eat, and proceed to enjoy the rest of your evening in a clean home, relaxing. How closely does this describe your life? What is the key difference between the two? Where do you want to be?

I think most of us would prefer the latter.

An Organized Home Is a Healthier, Safer Environment

No one thinks their home is dangerous, but a look at some statistics tells us this is not always the reality. Every year, more than 18,000 people in America die from accidental injuries that took place in the home. What does that mean? Apart from the cars on the road, it takes the solid place of the second-most-common location of accidental fatalities.

You might also not be happy to find out that

- **6,000 deaths** a year are caused by falls in the home, specifically in bathtubs or showers.
- **5,000 people** a year are killed by accidental poisoning, including people who are young and those who are of middle age.
- **3,000 lives** per year are claimed from accidental fires and burn-related injuries.
- **1,000 people** die each year from airway obstruction. Children, specifically, are at a much higher risk from these sorts of fatalities. It could be strangulation, choking, or even suffocation.
- **800 deaths** every year are caused by submersion and drowning, specifically among young children.

(Mullins, 2021)

Now, this is a rather grim and dreary start to a book that is meant to be about habits and gaining personal peace and freedom. However, this grim reality highlights a very important aspect of an organized home—safety. Think about it this way: Having a cluttered house is dangerous. Why? Because it can lead to avoidable accidents such as the ones listed above. As you can see, these are the reasons people can possibly suffer an accidental death in their very own house. Elderly people are at an even higher risk of accidents at home, especially tripping and falling.

Another example of when a disorganized home becomes unsafe is when someone has a gun collection but does not have a secure place to store their guns. If you have children, the necessity for proper and secure gun storage cannot be overstated. Too many tragic accidents have occurred for this matter to be ignored. A quick Google search heartbreakingly turns up over seven million results with headlines about children ranging from two to six years old accidentally shooting themselves.

Though somber and perhaps even dark, this is one very serious reason why an organized home is a necessity. Depending on how you manage things, a messy, disorganized home can lead to a wide variety of issues. One disturbing example is the boy who was not in the habit of cleaning his room but rather leaving items lying around and got bitten by a violin spider that had crawled into his sock on the floor. Yikes!

Too much clutter and items that are not put away in designated places can create a fire hazard. Just put batteries in the wrong place, for example. There are so many unexpected flammable items in the house. For instance, did you know that sugar is flammable? So are nail polish, mattresses, cooking oil, and dryer lint, the most common cause of dryer fires.

Even if they are not necessarily a fire hazard, pests seem to be especially attracted to an unorganized home. Homes with clutter are harder to clean, and unsanitary conditions can lead to illness and infection, which in turn can lead to greater overall health concerns.

A Messy Home Can Hinder Your Career

I often tell people that my room is a true reflection of my life. When there is chaos in my life, my room, too, is in chaos. When things are going well, my room seems to be much more orderly and inviting.

Unfortunately, the messiness in one's home can easily spill over into their workplace. For a supervisor, noticeable disorganization or dishevelment might be a warning sign to them, and they may end up overlooking you for promotions and advancements. Disorganization and chaos are two key factors that a workplace does not appreciate, and being organized might be even more important in some professions than others. For example, healthcare and medical professionals should have good organization skills because every detail, tool, piece of equipment, and even cotton pad needs to be accounted for.

It may be a harsh wake-up call for anyone trying to boost their career. A person might be excellent at their job, but you'd be surprised to learn how much the little details matter and have a domino effect on other aspects of their life. Just like a person has to suit up and appear presentable, so does their workspace and home in order to leave a lasting impression on their peers around them.

Clutter Can Affect Your Mental Health

A healthy life is a happy one, and the state of your home can certainly influence your overall mental health. Clutter has a nasty way of increasing a person's stress and can lead to greater feelings of fatigue. You might not even realize what the culprit is or the impact your environment is having on you. But think about it this way: You are driving down an open road, surrounded by rolling fields of sweeping grass and colorful flowers. Music blares from the radio as a fresh breeze fills the car.

Got the picture? Nice, isn't it? Now wipe it from your mind.

Now picture yourself driving in a traffic jam on the highway with cars on every side. It is peak rush hour, and the heat of the sun is beating down on you through the window. You can hardly hear your music for the constant honks of drivers anxious to get home. You clutch the steering wheel tighter, feeling tense despite knowing you will eventually arrive at your destination.

It paints a different picture, doesn't it? The former is filled with serenity, the latter with chaos. When it comes to matters of the home, this kind of stress can have a huge impact on you, even if you are not fully aware of the source of this oppressive amount of stress.

Anxiety is one of the key issues people are dealing with in this day and age. As the clutter accumulates in your home, stress accumulates in your mind. Your mental health should always be of high priority, so although you might not feel like cleaning today, you will ultimately feel better if you live in a clean and organized house.

Being Organized Is More Convenient

This benefit is perhaps not as important or noticeable as the others, but sometimes it's the little things that keep us moving forward. Anyone knows that once they have overslept, it is a race to get ready and find the items you need for your day as fast as possible before storming out the door, dashing towards the car while eating a protein bar, and thinking of a plausible excuse to give your boss for your tardiness. The more organized your house is, the less time you'll spend looking for misplaced items. Granted, the example given is a little extreme and is hopefully not a common occurrence for you, but how many times have you been rushing around to get out of the house only to spend five or ten precious minutes searching for your shoes or keys?

The more often you use items, the more often they can get lost, so having an organized system can save you time regardless of what the items are.

I have spent too much time in the kitchen looking for scissors, too much time in the study looking for pens, and heaven knows where that remote went in the living room, but the moment that an organized structure was put in place, finding these items and more around the house became much easier.

Can Save You Money

At first, you may feel as if getting organized is expensive rather than financially beneficial, especially if you need to fork over money for the storage items and other organizational gear, yet once you have more organized space, you will certainly end up spending less money in the long run. For example, grocery shopping is a regularly occurring big expense for every household. If you have a cluttered, disorganized kitchen, you may end up buying items you already have, adding unnecessary costs to your grocery bill. Or, for instance, you may need to buy specific items that you know you already have and desperately need for a task or project but cannot for the life you find in your house, leaving you no choice but to go out and buy a new one.

Sets a Good Example

If you happen to have kids, you're setting a great example for them by providing them with an upbringing in a clean and organized home. Your habits become their habits, and they will take those habits with them to their very own homes one day. This means that if you teach your kids proper cleaning, storage, and organizational habits and allow them to be a part of the whole process, they will learn to take care of and be responsible for their own belongings.

Greater Love for Your Home

Whether you work at home or have a daily commute, your house is your personal space, and you want a home that you love and feel comfortable in. When a place is disorganized, cluttered, or dirty, we often do not want to spend a lot of time in that space. You may find yourself looking for excuses to stay away from the mess. After a long, hard day of work, the majority of people want to come back to an environment where they can find comfort and peace. So the more organized your home becomes, the more freedom you will feel while spending time in your personal space.

Cleanliness Is Contagious

The more you start organizing different areas in your home, the more addictive it becomes, causing you to want to keep organizing! It can have a huge impact on anyone else who is currently living in your house, too, and you might even find people asking you for your advice so they can start to take steps toward being more organized in their own homes.

Your Self-Esteem Boost

Many matters in life are beyond our control, but you absolutely have control over your home. And best of all, it can make you want to invite others into your home so that they can enjoy it, too. You will always feel comfortable that your home is clean and organized, so even surprise visitors won't have you scrambling to pick up the laundry from the dining room table.

To put it simply, the best way to avoid feeling ashamed of your home and instead have confidence in its appearance and in yourself is to create a more organized space.

Keeping a space organized is not always the easiest habit for people to adopt, but the sooner they get it right, the more it can benefit them and everyone around them. When you are sharing a space with people, you want to make sure they share similar values to yours. Otherwise, it could put a dent in your plan to have an organized and well-sorted home.

Signs That Your Home Is an Unhealthy Place to Live

No one likes to stray into the realm of bad news. After all, who likes bad news? Even the question, "Do you want the bad news first or the good news first?" is enough to fill anyone with dread. Because, although there is good news, the promise of bad news takes over.

This is exactly why I always want to hear the bad news first because the good news might just bring some comfort. For now, this is a glimpse into the possibility that your home might just be an unhealthy environment to live in (and perhaps even the reason you picked up this book). You may not even be aware of what you are doing or not doing in your house that could actually be harmful to you and your family.

You first need to understand that home is where your health starts. It might take a while before you get around to dusting, or maybe you allow your pets to sleep in your bed, or maybe you can see much moisture building up on the bathroom windows.

All these factors seem innocent enough, but they and others could be making you and the other members of your household sick.

Here are some signs to look out for to determine if your home may have the potential to cause health issues:

- Your house might be retaining too much moisture in the wrong places. Although it's no secret that bathing and cooking can contribute to the buildup of moisture in the home, having too much of it is not safe because mold loves to grow in moist areas. The more humid the environment, the more mold is bound to grow. Mold tends to sprout up in corners and on ceilings and can cause throat irritation, coughing, nasal stuffiness, and more.

- You may be vacuuming without making use of a HEPA filter. Research has shown that air pollution nearly causes around 200,000 early deaths according to News, 2013, and it exacerbates allergies and asthma. Guess what is a common way of exposing yourself to air pollution? You guessed it—vacuum cleaners. You want to invest in a High-Efficiency Particulate Air (HEPA) filter vacuum. This prevents tiny dust particles from simply being blown back into the air indoors. Further, you need to remind yourself to change the vacuum filter from time to time, even if you are making use of a HEPA filter, especially if you start to notice that the filter is starting to wear and tear (*Study: Air Pollution*, 2013).

- Checking the cleanliness of vents is not exactly the first thing on a person's to-do list. A person might be more inclined to tackle the much more immediate problem of piled-up dirty dishes. However, they are still in need of cleaning as they can gather a whole lot of dust. When you turn on that air conditioner or furnace, that dust gets blown out of the vents and spread all over the house. You should be able to remove the vent covers in your home so you can clean all the dust and grime within your reach. However, it might be wise to get the help of a professional in order to get your ducts properly cleaned. Considering that professionals tend to use compressed air and air agitators to get rid of the hard-to-clean dust, they are simply equipped with better tools to do a more thorough job.

- Your bathroom might have poor ventilation. Are you keeping the window open or running the exhaust fan when you are taking a shower? If you're not, then you should start, because the extra moisture that occurs in the bathroom can expedite the mold growth inside your home, which can really damage your house as well as your health.
- You may be using the wrong household cleaners. If you are spraying cleaner all around your house, it is certainly going

to settle on a wide variety of surfaces, and you and your family are inhaling what you are spraying and touching those surfaces. Considering people are cleaning more than ever before since the pandemic, it is critical to make use of the right cleaners to prevent yourself from being exposed to harsh chemicals. Also remember that any harsh chemicals found in items like dish soap, bleach, and even bath products have the capability of damaging your airways and lungs. In fact, an investigation conducted by the Environmental Working Group determined that over 2,000 cleaning supplies contain substances linked to a wide variety of health problems such as asthma, allergies, and perhaps even cancer according to EWG, 2016.

- You are ignoring your gutters. When gutters have a buildup of materials such as leaves and sticks and become clogged, it can allow excess moisture to creep onto your walls, your crawl space, or your basement. If you do not have gutters that are covered, it is important for you to make sure they are cleaned on a regular basis.

- Even if you vacuum and dust the rooms of your house, it is important for you to move your couches, tables, beds, and other furniture away from the walls to properly clean them as well as under and around them. It is especially startling to see how much dust can collect at the bottom of furniture. You do not have to do it every day, but doing it every couple of months will certainly help.

- Wearing shoes inside the house is a common habit, especially among Americans. You may not be rolling around on the floor of a public bathroom, but you do walk inside them and then walk into your house with the exact same shoes. The same goes for literally everywhere you walk in your shoes. Depending on where you put your feet, you are bringing all of the dirt, grime, and germs your shoes have collected into your home and depositing it on the carpet your kids play on.

- Too much stuff in the home can actually contribute to poor air quality as it is constantly collecting dust, pollen, and dander. Unless you have the time to constantly move and clean the items, you should consider reducing your collection of furnishings.

Making Your Home a Priority

Let's start with the very first habit of the day—making your home a priority. You may now understand both the benefits that come with having an organized house and the potential harm that can come with having a messy home.

So you have decided you want to make your home organization a priority. What does that mean? It means you will be exerting extra effort toward creating a safe and healthy space within the walls of your home. It means that your house takes precedence over work, blogging, scrolling on social media, and other things that take up your time but don't necessarily create peace in your life.

Now that doesn't mean you should quit your job or give up your social life. It just means you need to bump your home life up the list a little bit.

For instance, I know for a fact that once I began living on my own, I did not prioritize the importance of the dishes over the time spent on Netflix. As the sink filled up and my kitchen became dirtier, I found I was "too tired" to deal with the mess. I did not realize that the mess was caused because I did not make it a priority.

In order to prioritize your home's cleanliness, you need to understand that

- Everything else happening in your life is in fact quite dependent on the state of your home. Considering that every day of your life begins and ends in your house, it makes sense that your mood, energy level, and health depend on the condition of the space you are living in.
- There is really a whole lot to do at home. People often feel that staying at home is boring or that a person took a job rather than staying at home because of the dull monotony. However, this is a false reality as there is always an endless amount of cleaning and organizing that can be done in the home.
- Roping in your family or housemates with you on your organization journey is

also incredibly important as they share your space and can contribute to its organization—or lack thereof. However, if you are living on your own, the responsibility to keep the house clean and organized falls only to you—which can be a good thing and a bad thing.

How to Convince Members of Your Household to Join Your Journey

If you are living on your own, the biggest challenge you will have to overcome is to convince yourself to stay structured and organized. If you are not living alone in a house, then this becomes even trickier because some people simply settle for the chaos, while others are all too keen to keep things neat. Obviously, you will be treating it a little differently if you are working with family members than if you are working with roommates.

How to Get Your Family to Stay Organized

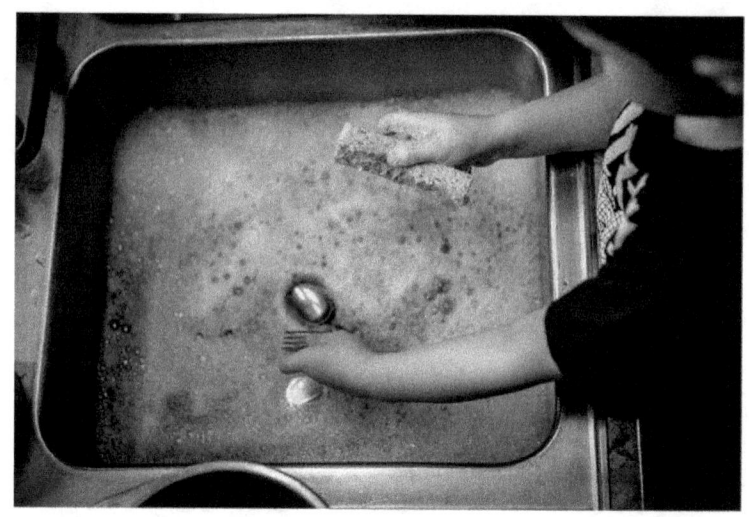

It isn't easy to always keep people invested in the same goals that you have. You will need some fresh ideas to help keep your family motivated to follow the new routines.

One of the first steps you need to take is making the mornings work for you. You want to leave yourself some time to wake up before you dive into all the other tasks that need to be completed in the morning. So what exactly can you do? For one, you can make some printable morning routine cards—this is an ideal way to have your children follow a more consistent morning routine. Challenge yourself to never have to say, "Hurry up!" as you walk out the door. Why? Well, hurrying up and rushing the morning routine can actually raise stress levels and ultimately does not aid in time management or punctuality.

As the adult in the situation, your behavior in the household will have powerful effects on the other family members.

Create Designated Spaces

In order to create an organized home, you all need to work together as a team, so why not have designated places for all the items your family needs to efficiently go about their daily routines? For example, school bags and shoes can be kept in crates or on shelves close to the door.

Create a Visual Weekly Schedule

Once you have a visual schedule and place it in a prominent spot, everyone in the house can clearly see what needs to be done each day. Having the activities that all family members take part in is great for keeping the whole family organized, and keeping a list of the chores and who is responsible for each can remove the excuse of "I didn't know it was my turn." Whenever schedules become visible, they act as an immediate reminder and can help your kids learn to become more independent.

You can direct your children and other family members to the schedule every morning so that they can review everything that needs to be done.

Set Up for Success

You'll want to identify the areas that are problematic or not running as smoothly as they could within the routine and try to find simple solutions to make the tasks less complicated. For example, having your children lay out their school clothes the night before allows them to get dressed quickly in the morning, and you can even help your kids develop a system for storing their clothes. Setting up a homework box makes it easier for the kids to find their completed homework and make sure it makes its way into their book bags. If your kids need to clean, then setting up a cleaning kit that they can access on their own is quite a clever idea.

Cleaning Routine

You should not be the only one cleaning the house. You are sharing a space with people, so therefore, it is everyone's responsibility to keep their own space as well as shared spaces clean and clutter-free. This means you need to get the kids and other family members involved in the household tasks, whether it be cleaning, cooking, or other tasks that might feel like chores. Granted, your children may not complete the tasks in the same way you would, but you will be teaching your kids very important life skills by putting the responsibility of certain chores or tasks on them. Here are some tips to get your kids involved in household work:

- Create and maintain chore charts.
- Have designated spots and storage areas for items to go such as shelves, baskets, and crates.
- Involve your children in dividing up the tasks and keeping track of their completion on the chore charts.

Prioritize What Is Important for Your Family

Each family has different ideas of how to best run their household. If you know what is important to you and your family, you can determine what tools and systems you'll need in order to achieve your organizational goals by choosing what is likely to be most effective in your home.

How to Keep an Organized House With Roommates

This is perhaps a little trickier as you may not have the same kind of authority as you would within a family household. One way to maintain a clean and organized home when living with roommates is to draw up a contract stating agreed-upon rules and systems for keeping the house clean.

Everyone obviously has their own way of doing things, but you really want to make your expectations clear from the start before sharing a home with someone. Although this cannot erase all troubles, it is certainly one way to mitigate possible future issues.

Some suggestions when dealing with a messy roommate are

- Explain to them what is causing your distress. Communication is very important regardless of the relationship with your roommate. Instead of tossing around accusations, you need to clearly and calmly explain yourself. Tell them that you want to propose some changes and invite them to help you out. This may involve you simply stating that you have concerns and asking for your roommate's help in addressing the problems.

- Pick your battles. No one likes to get nitpicked, so you have to really choose what exactly you want to voice your opinion on. This means you might not be able to point out every single dirty dish that has been left in the sink or every single sock left on the floor. Instead, focus on the bigger issues that really affect the living space. For instance, if your roommate has forgotten to put away their laundry and instead left it lying around in a common space, you might want to give them a gentle reminder, which will hopefully result in a quick apology and the removal of clothes from the living room.
- You can also ask to have your items kept separately. It can go a long way for you to establish boundaries in the house. You can determine which spaces are theirs, which are yours, and which will be communal together. If you find that the clutter of your roommate starts to creep

into your space, you can remind them of the boundaries you determined together, or you can move the items of theirs that are in your space into their designated space. You cannot do much about what your roommate does with their bedroom unless, of course, it becomes a health issue.

- You can also suggest having a chore list. This is a battle you will have to pick at some point—how exactly do you go about telling your roommate to clean the bathroom? Very few people enjoy this task, and even asking someone to do so may feel like a chore in itself. Instead, ask for your roommate's help in coming up with a list of both daily and weekly chores that includes who is responsible for what. You can create a visual chore list and have tasks assigned to each person; you can alternate on who does certain unpleasant chores. It would not be fair for one person to always be stuck on bathroom duty.

- You can also agree to a pre-determined time during which you all clean together. Simply switch on some music and work on organizing and decluttering everything together, specifically in the rooms that you share. This is one way cleaning can be more fun and feel less like a boring chore.

These strategies can help save relationships with messy roommates while also making your home a whole lot more organized and efficient. Granted, it is certainly tougher having to share a home than living on your own when it comes to keeping the home clean and organized, but at the same time, sharing a home with others can also bring many benefits that people living on their own do not get to experience.

The goal is to take a diplomatic approach in order to help curb bad habits, but remember to keep your own expectations in check and that you can't control the actions of others.

Key Principles to Consider

- Having a cluttered house can make your living environment dangerous.
- Your quality of life and that of those who share your house will greatly improve through implementing an organized and functional system.
- You will have to get the people with whom you share your home on board with your goals in order for your strategy to work.

Thoughts for Reflection

- How much clutter is in your house?
- Are there any spaces in your house that are potentially dangerous due to clutter?
- Do you feel like the chaos inside your home controls you, or do you have control over the chaos?
- What are three steps you can take today to start becoming more organized?

HABIT 2: CREATE A SYSTEM AROUND YOUR HOME THAT WORKS FOR YOU

One thing I always remember when I think about organizational management systems is this one time when I walked into a crowded, musty shop. I could not tell whether the store had the item I was looking for and because the cashier was busy watching TV, I did not feel free to ask. I spent a good while wandering the aisles trying to make sense of the system they had going. Eventually, I did find what I was looking for, but I left the shop later shaking my head.

I remember then walking into another shop to buy an air fryer. An employee approached me and I showed him a picture of what I was looking for. He walked me over to the air fryer, placed it in my cart, and added a sticker to make it easier to pay at the register. After completing my transaction, a store employee walked to my car with me and loaded the heavy item. To say I was impressed, especially because my concern was dropping the expensive item, was the understatement of the year.

But how on earth does the way a business is run have any reflection on how a household is run? Well, I think a house works a whole lot like a business. Tasks need to be completed within a specific amount of time, stock needs to be taken into consideration, and rules are set in place to make sure everything runs properly.

What Exactly Is Home Management?

House management, or home management, is a term you will hear a lot when you are working to organize your own home and one that we will frequently use in this book. It basically refers to keeping your house in general order with only a limited amount of time to do so.

But do you understand what exactly house management truly entails?

Good home management means keeping your household running effectively. It involves all aspects from cleaning and keeping track of events and activities to taking care of pets and maintaining a budget. You will want to delegate the necessary responsibilities to the other family members and make sure that these tasks are taken care of when the time comes.

So why is home management so important?

Home management will make just about everything else in your life flow better. After all, everything starts at home—your meals, your career, your family, your health, your hobbies, and more. When you find a method to run your household efficiently, everything else will begin to naturally fall in place.

If you are not stressing about every single task or chore, then you might also find yourself with some free time—though many people might be wondering if such a thing actually exists. I can assure you it does, and it is wonderful. Having a well-kept and organized home allows you the freedom to choose to take a break without being overwhelmed by tasks that need to be done when your break is over.

Because, in reality, we all need to take a break once in a while. But the reality of chores, tasks, pressures, and sometimes even soccer balls flying over our heads gets in the way of achieving that peace of mind that we need.

Steps to Start Organizing Your Home

Most everyone has a unique profession outside of their homes, but inside, most of us also have to do the same cooking, cleaning, decorating, driving others around, organizing, playing nurse and referee, and even stitching up torn clothes from time to time.

Although people appreciate it when someone is a master of a certain skill, when living in a home, it is sometimes necessary to be a jack of all trades. Instead of struggling to juggle tasks in a way that causes stress, you need to create for yourself a great home management system that works well for your specific needs.

So just how do you go about creating a home management system? To start, you need to be realistic, especially when you share your home with others. You only have so much time in a day, and even so, you don't want to book all the time up with cleaning and tending to different housework. As much as the benefits of keeping your house neat will certainly improve your life, the goal is for it to benefit you—not control you. Funny how easy it can be to cross that line. Life is all about balance, including how exactly you go about running your house.

Start by Creating a List

Pop off that pen cap and grab a piece of paper—it's time to make a plan. In order to create a great plan, you need to know and understand all the tasks that need to get done, so start by writing down all the chores that need to be completed

- every day
- every week
- every month
- every year

Draw up a list that makes sense for you and your family and the amount of time you have to dedicate to home tasks. It can be really easy to go overboard when listing the chores and tasks, but try to keep this list down to the bare minimum. Everything on this list should be essential to running a clean, safe, and organized household. For instance, tasks such as paying the bills, running errands, cooking and baking, and other necessary administrative-type work should be included as these are the tasks you need to complete in order to live and therefore should be a part of your home management system.

Adopting a Routine

Routines—as dull as they might sound for some and as glorious for others—are a vital part of achieving and maintaining tidiness in your home. If you regularly follow your routines, you will find that even the biggest challenges are easier to overcome. For example, say it's time to cook supper; this job is much easier to accomplish if you don't walk in to find that all your pots are dirty and the sink is filled with dishes. If you have a routine of loading and running the dishwasher in the morning, you might find it's much easier to begin, and therefore complete, the task of cooking supper.

Another family I know has the routine of alternating whose turn it is to clean the dishes every week. Each week, one person is responsible for making sure the dishes are clean and ready to use for the entire week. Although it might be quite a hassle for that individual, in a family of four, each person only has to worry about ensuring there are clean dishes available for one week, but they always get to enjoy the fact that clean dishes are always available when they need them.

This is merely an example of a system that generally works well. But, of course, there are always exceptions. For example, a person who works different shifts and hours or lives a lifestyle that demands flexibility might be incapable of adopting a proper routine, and in turn, their home life might suffer if they are not careful. However, this person might then simply consider adopting a realistic to-do list that they update on a regular basis—in this way, they can keep track of what needs to be done but won't feel pressured to get those things done at a certain time.

Morning and Evening Routines

The morning and evening routines are all about what you need to do every morning and every evening. These are the steps you take to get your days started and the steps you take to get your house right back in order at the end of the day.

Weekly Cleaning Routines

This is a list of all the cleaning tasks you want to accomplish each day of the week. It can be as simple as spending around 15 to 20 minutes each day cleaning a very specific part of your house that does not require deep cleaning.

The majority of people have reverted to cleaning the entire house on the weekends when they are not at work. However, deep cleaning an entire house all in one day (depending on the size and other pertinent factors) can consume a whole lot of the time meant for you to relax and rejuvenate. But once you switch up your cleaning schedule into more manageable chunks, you have more freedom and flexibility to move things around, giving you and your family more time to spend together on the weekends.

To start off with a weekly routine, you will want to consider the best times to complete smaller routines such as laundry, paperwork, and meal planning and prepping. Divide necessary cleaning throughout the seven days of the week and leave yourself one or two days to either have completely off or to catch up on what you might have missed during the week.

Adding a Deep Cleaning Routine

This will be the last component within the house management. Deep cleaning is all about dividing your house into cleaning zones. Your kitchen can be one cleaning zone, the bathrooms another, the master bedroom another, and so on until each part of your house is part of a zone. You want a system where you will deep clean those areas at least once a month. Naturally, again, this will depend entirely on the size of your house.

But wait! It is not the end of the world if you cannot manage this because of your lifestyle or time constraints. Remember that we are trying to be realistic here. In that case, consider creating something like a quarterly deep cleaning schedule for chores that need to be done regularly but not necessarily often. You will need to list all the tasks you need to do for deep cleaning in your house, and you will perform them on a quarterly basis so that you are not tied to a very specific zone or a very specific order of cleaning.

Why would this work better? Because some tasks in the house and in the rooms will take more time than others. One day, you might realize you might have two hours free where you can dive into the kitchen and deep clean the oven. On another day, you might only have twenty minutes, and so you decide to spend that time wiping the fridge clean because even the fridge needs to be cleaned from time to time.

Installing House Management Systems

You might have to re-evaluate all the tasks that need to be done on a regular basis. Here are some other tasks for you to consider:

- grocery shopping
- cleaning the floors
- laundry
- budgeting and paying bills
- meal planning and prepping
- record-keeping

Now that you have identified the primary areas that need to be worked on in your house, you should do your best to design a system—a system with the goal of running your household is truly the best and most effective way.

For instance, let's consider meal planning and meal prepping. You will have to think about which day of the week will be best for you to set aside time to plan your meals. You also want to consider whether or not you want to plan your meals for an entire month, just one week at a time, or perhaps even every few days. Would you like to have the same options for breakfast every day for a whole week, or would the rest of your family prefer to have a couple of options to choose from throughout the week?

Once you have figured out the day you want to do your meal planning, you can think of the best way to form your meal plan. It could involve matters like

- seeing what items you already have at home
- looking at Pinterest recipe boards for new ideas
- considering the amount of time you have each day to cook dinner
- seeing what you can do to prep for meals ahead of time

Now, as much as I wish I could leave you with a perfect step-by-step system, the reality is that each household is different and will require different things to run smoothly. This means that no formula created by someone who lives in a different household will fit yours perfectly. It also means that it is going to take some trial and error, but at the end of the day, it will be a huge time saver. You will start to appreciate how the household is being managed far more efficiently.

House Management Checklists

Another tool for managing your household is checklists. Checklists are both fun and fulfilling, and if you are already a fan of to-do lists, then you will certainly love their cousin, the checklist. Checklists are designed to be helpful with big projects in your house and events that you are planning. You can use checklists for things like

- vacation planning
- party planning
- holiday planning
- spring cleaning
- home improvements
- decluttering projects

The idea is for you to create a checklist for yourself not only to help you remember all the steps in a task or project but also to keep track of your overall progress. You can even save your checklists to refer back to the next time you need them for a similar task.

The beauty of living in the digital era is the availability of apps of all kinds on your smartphone, or you can type up a checklist with your preferred word processing program and print it out each time when you have an upcoming event. It's simple to do, and you can even just press TAB in order to make subtasks under the big tasks:

- clear out the decorations in the garage
- start with box A
- start with box B
- deal with the dusty glass decorations in box B

If you want to revert back to another big task, all you need to do is simply press enter again.

*Tip: If you decide to make use of an app, make sure it is one that can be interconnected with your computer and your phone. Sometimes it might be easier to type up your to-do list, but if you are out getting organizational or cleaning supplies, it's very handy to have that list easily accessible on your smartphone. You can also choose to make use of either free or paid versions of certain apps. One of the best to-do list apps I have seen is called Clickup. You can easily work with the paid or the free version, depending upon which one you are most comfortable with.

Building a Binder

A home management binder, or file, is a handy tool when you want to keep all your house management information in one easily accessible place. The binder can be used to keep track of all your routines and systems, and it helps keep things organized.

A binder might seem a little over the top, but sometimes that is what is needed in order to achieve your household organization goals. It's okay to try out different ways to organize and use your binder until you find what works for you.

How to Make a Binder for Home Management

Don't worry, I'm not leaving you in the dark here! Here is a small guide you can follow in order to create your own binder, add the different categories and tabs, and make it your personal home manual.

The general idea of a binder is to grab a folder or 3-ring binder, print out the necessary pages, and start using it. They are actually quite simple to create, but they do require a little time and effort to pull together. However, you will be reaping the benefits of this small time investment for many years to come.

Step 1: Gather Everything You Need

You can't have a binder without actually owning a binder, so it is best to start off by putting together a little shopping list. It should not take a huge bite out of your wallet, but the following are some items to consider including:

- a folder or 3-ring binder
- dividers/tabs
- hole punch that coincides with your folder/binder style and size

- pens of different colors—you can color-code different rooms/zones, tasks, or even family members/roommates!
- blank paper or notepad
- label maker to label the tabs that are dividing your binder up
- checklists/printables—there are lots of amazing checklist templates available, or you can create your own personalized templates

Step 2: Making Use of Home Contents in a Binder

You will have a whole lot of information that will need to be kept inside your home file, so you want to create plenty of sections in order to easily locate items or information. This is when a label maker can come in handy; it can make the binder appear neater and tidier, and you can use it for your main headings.

What Should Be in a Home Management Binder?

You can divide your home file into different sections. You'll want to think about the categories your household and family would require and create a section for each. Here are examples of six common home binder sections:

- chores
    - the laundry schedule
    - chores checklist (such as the daily, deep cleaning, weekly, etc.)
    - quick-clean checklist
    - how to clean items
    - checklist for others
- family and friends' information
    - personal information such as shoe and clothing sizes, medical history and medications, hobbies/activities, etc.
    - information about your pets
    - family meeting notes and goals
    - babysitter information and any other home employees (house cleaner, landscaper, etc.)
    - party events
    - emergency information (if the worst happens)
    - address book
- food
    - shopping lists

- fridge, freezer, pantry lists
  - meals everyone loves
  - meal planners
  - allergies/food preferences
- house maintenance
  - to-do lists
  - to-buy list
  - maintenance calendar
  - home inventory list (in case your house gets robbed)
  - tech info
  - list of recommended tradespeople or those you have used and were happy with in the past
  - car maintenance and breakdown info
  - what should be done in a home emergency
- finances
  - debt tracker
  - savings tracker
  - household budget info
  - gift & card budget
  - bill tracker
  - spending tracker

- wish list
- in case of a stolen purse or bag—list what was inside
- account cheat sheet
* holidays and vacations
  - holiday ideas
  - packing lists
  - holiday planner
  - what to do when away
  - shopping list
  - staycation ideas
  - pre-holiday checklist
  - looking after kids (info for babysitters)
  - taking care of home info
  - taking care of pets info

Alright! Now you have a good idea of the kind of information you can place in your home binder. Of course, you can choose what to include and personalize it accordingly. However, you should avoid keeping vital paperwork in your home management binder:

- birth certificates
- passports

- insurance certificates
- car titles

Your home management binder should only involve matters of your home and of the family.

Step 3: Have a Nice Cover Page

Create your own personalized cover page that will be placed on the front. Basically, adding some decorations or making it look neat and pretty just adds to the appeal of your home binder, helps you customize it further, and allows things to look professional and last a whole lot longer.

Step 4: Adding the Plastic Files

You want to add plastic page protectors in order to place your planner sheets inside. It's a good idea to use the plastic sheet protectors as you might be displaying those planners later on clipboards hung on the wall or stuck to the fridge with a magnet. Either way, holes on the actual page don't really look so pretty or neat and can tear easily, and the plastic files can help keep them usable and looking nicer longer because sometimes the subtle details do indeed matter.

It also keeps the paper in a much better condition and makes it quicker to flick through the binder when you are hurriedly looking for something. You can also print extra sheets (such as meal plan templates, chore charts, party or holiday checklists, etc.) and keep them all in the exact same place with a nice plastic sleeve.

Step 5: Add All the Planner Pages in the Right Places in the Binder

You want to get it right the first time and make sure you place all the pages in places that make sense and are easy to locate later. A good rule of thumb is to draw up a table of contents guide to help you set the whole system up properly. It works a little bit like a textbook, except it is your personalized planning machine.

Step 6: Remember to Fill in the Necessary Information About You on the Pages

Now, this is what is likely going to take the most time as you are tackling matters all to do with running your home. However, now you can get rid of all the rest of the paper and to-do lists that lie scattered around the house. Imagine how freeing it will be once you have gotten rid of the noticeboard scattered with business cards and leaflets or when you don't have to stress about all the piles of paper and information. Once you have the home file up and running, all excess information scattered around can be tossed (just be sure to double-check every paper before tossing it and consider shredding informational papers if they happen to contain sensitive information).

And finally, take a deep breath, sit back, and know that you have set up for yourself a great and effective system to help you run the house.

Keep in mind that the tips and strategies in this book are all just suggestions. If you personally don't want to make a binder or don't think it will work for you, that is perfectly okay!

How to Start With Home Management Systems

Now we are backpedaling a little and returning to home management systems and how to get things moving. When you first start off, it can be overwhelming and difficult to know where to start, so you do not have to plan and implement everything all at once. You want to start by adding one routine or system at a time.

Start With the Areas Causing the Most Trouble

The best way of starting your home management system is to tackle the biggest problem areas in your home first. If you are unsure of where to start, take a moment to walk around and observe the areas of your house. Think about how many people are using a given space at any point and jot down which space has caused the most frustrations so far.

I often find myself eyeing the kitchen counter where clutter seems to congregate or my desk where dust seems to be attracted like magnets.

You need to find a place to start, so consider asking yourself some questions: How busy and chaotic are the mornings in your house? Does the question of what to have for supper stress you out every night? Do you always find yourself running to the stores for missing items or because you are running out of essential items? Does remaining within the budget seem nearly impossible?

Depending on how you answered these questions, you'll be able to address the most pressing problem areas first. These are the areas that cause you the most stress and take away from your time to get other things done or just to relax and enjoy your home.

Remember to Take It One Step at a Time

You can't take on all the problems in your life and expect to overcome them all in one go. We are humans after all, and as much as we wish we could load all the "tasks" and "skills" in our brains as they did in *The Matrix*, reality, unfortunately, does not work that way.

You want to tackle the problem areas, but do so one at a time. Give yourself the necessary space to fully implement changes and tweak those changes according to what works for your family's overall needs. If you do find yourself moving on to the next matter before you have completely adopted the previous system, you are setting yourself up to struggle with both.

If you created a home binder, be sure to keep it updated as you implement and tweak routines and systems. As a friend once told me, "Although it might feel like nothing changes, everything does change so quickly—it's hard to keep up." I could not agree more; in fact, it made me consider how quickly time has passed and what steps I have taken to adapt my routines to those changes. When you are working with a binder, you have to make an extra mental effort to keep track of the changes — even jotting things down in a small notebook if need be.

The Secret to Creating a Routine

Did you know that around 80% of Americans feel like they are stuck in their routine—whether good or bad (*80% of Americans*, 2017)?

But how does one go about starting a morning or an evening routine? It is not as simple as you might think. But the thing is, you already have a morning routine. The question is how effective is it?

Your goal is to remove the bad habits within your current routine and implement good habits that make your routine more effective and efficient. Mind you, it is going to be tough in the beginning, but a little bit of willpower can go a long way. Here are some steps to take to accomplish this feat:

- Decide what needs to be done in your morning routine. As you start implementing your new home management system, you will begin to identify what needs to be done as you wake up and prepare to face the day.
- Set small goals for yourself. For instance, on the first day maybe you start by drinking a full glass of water, then the next day you drink the water and add in making your bed. A big goal is very exciting to take on, but by creating smaller goals that can be accomplished daily, you are setting yourself up to be more successful in achieving the big goal.
- Be prepared for your new routine. You want to have all the pieces of the puzzle before you start. This makes it easier to keep going without having any kinds of

delays. For instance, if you decide you want to keep your desk space clean all year long, then start off by organizing everything on and in your desk. Be sure you have any organizational tools you'll want like small baskets or containers, paper trays, or pencil cups first, then you can focus on remembering to place everything back where it belongs every evening. You can then wipe your table and desk area every morning to get rid of any dust.

- Try to make it fun. Having someone join you on your organizational journey is a positive kind of peer pressure and can be more effective than relying on self-motivation alone. Self-motivation, although very important for success in life, can do with a little bit of help here and there. Implement a reward system for yourself. Fan of chocolate? Each time you successfully complete three or four tasks, reward yourself with a small bite of chocolate.
- Keep track of your progress regularly. Create a very clear visual calendar where you have marked everything that you

have achieved each day. This is a little bit of a psychological trick as many people would hate to break the chain of productivity and success that they have started for themselves.

- Remember to give yourself a well-deserved reward. Once you have fallen into a routine and are maintaining it consistently, then you can focus on rewarding yourself with a little bit of fun. For instance, if your goal was to clear the clutter from the floor every night, once you have successfully and consistently implemented this change, buy yourself a new pair of slippers that you can really enjoy wearing around the clean and decluttered house. You know what you like and enjoy, so choose a reward that will feel like a little gift to yourself. There is really nothing wrong with treating yourself for the small victories in life. After all, small victories tend to lead to bigger ones.

Small Tips for a Good Morning Routine

Having a morning routine is perhaps the most important in comparison to all the other routines. The morning often sets the precedent for how the rest of the day is going to go. Have you ever had the kind of day where you wake up all groggy, fail to eat breakfast, and go about with your hair still tangled or your teeth unbrushed? Even if you attend to these things later, you still have that ominous, wrong-footed sense that nothing has been completed.

Here are some tips for your morning routine:

- Do your best to get a good night's sleep. Sleep is essential for a person's energy, focus, and productivity. In order to achieve this, a person will have to learn to wind down at the end of the day, switch off the TV, and set an alarm as needed. These techniques will help you to get your needed seven to eight hours of sleep every night.
- Avoid hitting that snooze button. Snooze buttons were invented for comfort but not for practicality—or punctuality! Snooze buttons can be detrimental to your morning routine. What may have been intended as five minutes of extra sleep may very well turn into half an hour. The more you allow yourself to hit

the snooze button, the more difficult it will be to stop.
    - One strategy you can try to break the habit of snoozing is counting to five and forcing yourself to get out of bed in order to start your day.
    - Keep your slippers and a glass of water close to your bed. This gives you a small nudge to get out of bed because you're likely thirsty, and the slippers will make the chilly floor less daunting.
- Allow yourself enough time to get to work without being in a flustered rush. Whether you work from home or commute to an office, if you do not give yourself enough time to prepare, it can really add to the overall stress of the morning. This is especially true if you do not consider yourself to be a morning person.
- Stay hydrated and drink a full glass of water. Ironic how a book about effective habits reminds you to drink water, but then again, water is a critical component of having a great morning routine, not to mention good health in general. When

you focus on your health, you will feel the effects through extra energy, decreased headaches, and increased productivity.

- Enjoy a good cup of coffee or tea as you wake up in the morning. For many of us, a hot cup of coffee or tea while waking up can really make all the difference in the world. It makes your day more enjoyable before you have to sink your teeth into management and efficiency tasks scheduled for the day.

- Make room for self-care. Make sure you eat a healthy breakfast and attend to basic hygiene needs. A few minutes of a small self-care routine can support your overall happiness and well-being. Your morning self-care routine might include things like grooming, a skincare regimen, a shower, or reading a book or the newspaper in order to help you to relax. Yes, efficient management should involve self-care because the better you feel about yourself, the likelier you are to be motivated to get the other, more grinding tasks done for the day.

- If you can, try to fit in a quick workout. This will also put you in better spirits, increase your health, and boost your energy.
- Spend some time reviewing and prioritizing the different tasks you need to accomplish that day, and if you have a binder, this is a great time to whip it out and review what needs to be done.

How to Implement a Deep Cleaning Routine

Why does everything seem to need a deep cleaning? How can you deep clean every room in your house? Here are some tips for implementing a deep cleaning routine:

- Declutter everything before you start a deep clean. Either find a new place for the visible clutter or if you do not use it, consider getting rid of it as visible clutter does not belong in any room. When you clear the clutter, it makes the task of deep cleaning much easier.
- Focus on starting high and working your way down by tackling the larger, harder-

to-reach surfaces first such as the
- ceiling
- trim of the ceiling
- light fixtures
- tops of furniture and cabinets

You can clean these high-up surfaces using a microfiber mop or expandable duster. A good rule of thumb is to add a spritz of white vinegar to a bit of dish soap in order to prevent mildew and mold.

- Start moving down by next deep cleaning the windows. Windows are pretty easy to clean: using the hose attachments, vacuum the sills and the track then use glass cleaner to wipe the window from top to bottom.

  You might want to save yourself some trouble by taking down the blinds or shades to more easily access the window itself. You can vacuum blinds using the brush attachment or toss curtains in the wash. If you do not want to launder or iron them, then you can simply fluff them up in the dryer for a couple of minutes as you wipe the rings and rods.

Then you can hang them right back up and continue.

- Try to remove as much dust as you can from hard surfaces using a soft cloth. If you want it to go even quicker, you can use a clean cotton tube sock over hand to dust the different surfaces as you move the objects to be dusted around with your other hand.
- Last but not least, it's time to deep clean the floors. This might mean moving larger pieces of furniture such as the sofas and beds. If you do not live alone, then this might be time to call the troops and have them help you move the furniture

*Bonus tip: Please use your legs and not your back whenever you are moving large or heavy items. You want to stay as safe as possible and avoid any trips to the ER.

What Are Some Tools to Help With Deep Cleaning?

Cleaning tools are necessary for effective cleaning. Here are some suggested tools to make your cleaning easier and more effective:

- clean paint brushes
- dish soap
- gloves
- baking soda
- rubbing alcohol
- streak-free window/glass cleaner
- distilled white vinegar
- lint roller
- microfiber cloths

This may seem like a long and overwhelming list, but remember that everything in this book, from the morning routine to the home binder and cleaning tools to the management system, are just suggestions. You should feel free to tweak these suggestions in ways that fit you and your home best. No one knows your life better than you do, so making adjustments to see what works best for you is not only a possibility, it is recommended!

Key Principles to Consider

- Draw up a list of all the tasks that need to be completed on a daily, weekly, monthly, and yearly basis.
- Design a plan and create a binder in order to keep track of all your necessary home tasks and to help others find the key information they need to know.
- Start the implementation of a home management routine as quickly as possible.

Thoughts for Reflection

- Do you have a morning routine? If so, what do you normally get done first? Is your current routine working for you?
- Do you understand all the tasks that need to be accomplished, or do other people constantly have to remind you?
- How many people can help you out in your home? What are they willing to do? What should be their responsibility?
- Do you think a binder will help you to keep track of everything that needs to get

done in the house?

HABIT 3: KEEPING THINGS IN THE HOME SIMPLE

Human beings by nature seem to love to overcomplicate matters when they are delving into the home. When it comes to running and managing places, the one thing I have learned is the simpler, the better.

Why? Because simpler management tactics just make life's little tasks easier and quicker. For example, you might not think that labeling makes things simpler, but it cuts down the time people spend looking for things, and they don't have to ask where things belong. We go deeper into the practice of labeling in chapter 10.

So how do you go about simplifying your home and therefore simplifying your life? Do you need a detailed step-by-step plan? Well, yes and no. Think about it this way, imagine you are on a weight-loss journey and you are using a program. Some programs are extremely restrictive, which means you have to go over and beyond with planning and recipes. You appreciate the restrictions as they are strict yet simple to understand. On the other hand, this may cause you more stress because you do not have the space or time to plan the meals of a restrictive diet. Rather, you would prefer to stick to more flexible rules of eating because it works better for your lifestyle and personality.

Keeping things in your home simple is largely defined by what you believe to be simple.

When it comes to your home, there are a couple of tactics that you can implement to slowly get your home organized.

Every day, take the time to establish a couple of essential daily rhythms, which are the tasks in the household that have to be done every day in order for your house to function smoothly. For example, having someone load and run the dishwasher in the evenings and having another unload it in the mornings generally helps to keep the kitchen functioning. Essential daily rhythms do not have to be completed at specific times or even in a specific order, but they do help you to feel like your house is manageable and under control.

Determining your daily rhythms will depend on you, your family, your preferences, and your lifestyle. So take your time in considering the bare minimum of what you would like to see get done every day. It could be starting the morning with one load of laundry, wiping the bathroom and kitchen counters, or whatever you need to keep the day moving. Evening rhythms generally involve the quick tidying up after the day's activities.

Allow your house to "reset" once or twice a day. This is when you take a couple of minutes to quickly tidy up your house and put things away at specific times in the day. This is the baseline of neatness you would like to maintain in your house. The plan is to do this once or twice a day to return your house to the baseline. The idea is not to spring clean your house once or twice a day but to help maintain a level of tidiness and organization that allows you to continue with your other daily activities.

The best way to maintain a house is to clear the clutter and keep possessions to a minimum. When you own fewer items, there is going to be a decreased amount of mess in your home. This also means your daily resets will be easier and quicker. One strategy to manage clutter is to be a clutter gatekeeper. What does this mean? Always be on the lookout and clear any piles threatening to become clutter.

Work on getting more organized. It might feel like you're adding more work to your plate and complicating matters, but there is nothing simple about chaos. Sometimes the process of simplifying matters at home requires you to first get things organized. It is a lot easier to keep things in your home tidy when it is organized. Makes sense, right? The more you declutter, the easier it also is to stay organized. So basically, the most complicated and difficult aspect of this is getting started. The more you dive into organizing, the easier matters will get over time.

Make use of the "one touch" rule, which can be another habit to get into to simplify your home and your life. The aim of this rule is to touch things once and put them right back after using them. The thinking behind this is "do not put it down, just put it away." The more you find yourself following this rule, the easier it will be to keep your house neat and organized, and other people in your household can also follow this rule to keep the space tidy. However, no one is going to follow this rule perfectly, so make sure your expectations are reasonable as you and the people sharing your home are likely to forget from time to time.

Another useful strategy is "brain dumps." Most people walk about with an ever-growing to-do list in their heads. There is always something that needs to get done, errands to be run, and critical dates that need to be remembered. It is a whole bunch of stuff to keep track of, which is not only exhausting, but it's also way too easy to forget things!

So every morning (add it into your morning routine!), take a couple of minutes to write down all the tasks that need to get done that day—or "dump" all your thoughts into a checklist or to-do list. It will help you clear the thoughts swirling around your head, and you won't have to worry about forgetting anything.

The moment you have gotten everything down on paper, you can prioritize the tasks. You want to focus on what needs to get done first and remove tasks that are not actually as necessary if you know you won't have time to do them.

Prioritize Your Time

Did you know that, according to the American Time Use Survey conducted by the US Bureau of Labor in 2021, on an average day, women spend around 2.7 hours on household activities and men spend around 2.2 hours? Those are large chunks of the day dedicated to maintaining a household, so it's important to prioritize tasks to fit them in each day.

Remember that once you have gotten everything written down, you will want to figure out when exactly you will have time to accomplish each task. It can be very helpful to get your top three priorities sorted for each day, then focus on all the other aspects and tasks. I admit that it can be tough to start with the higher-priority tasks because they are often the most difficult and time-consuming tasks. However, once they are out of the way, then the remaining tasks and chores become much easier.

Even though you are planning your day-to-day tasks, you will benefit from planning your week as a whole. Planning your week gives you an idea of the bigger picture. Think of what is happening in the week ahead and what tasks you would like to accomplish. This can help you avoid forgetting or missing other important matters in your schedule which could leave you feeling overwhelmed, stressed, or overscheduled.

Once you start doing these brain dumps and choosing three top priorities for each day of the week, then you can figure out all the other tasks and activities and when you'll have time for them.

How to Avoid Overscheduling

Picture this: 27-year-old Mia kept working long and hard for a company. She was scaling up the ladder as a businesswoman and had a packed schedule. She received a phone call from her mother who told her that she had not seen her in over a year.

Shocked and appalled, Mia decided to take a look at her schedule, and to her horror, she was booked for the next three months. She realized something needed to change.

Mia then started delegating some tasks to her coworkers, and she started saying no to tasks she knew she really did not have time for. Soon, she managed to find time to spend with her mother and friends, and her relationships radically improved.

Admit it, we are all guilty of this to some degree. I remember the time my eager-beaver self sat down and jotted down all my chores. I always think I'll have far more time than I ever actually do. Perhaps this is due to my overly enthusiastic personality, or perhaps it is because the to-do list never seems to end. But by the end of the day, overscheduling leads to far more problems, overcomplicates matters, and leaves you right back where you started because overscheduling can eventually lead to burnout.

Buffer Zones

Start off by scheduling activities and deadlines with a "buffer zone." This means you should give yourself 15 to 30 minutes between tasks and activities in case something ends up taking more time than you think it will. Scheduling things back-to-back can cause a whole lot of stress, and although many people do it, it's not altogether a very realistic approach. This is particularly true for meetings, where a person often has some preparation or role. Booking meetings back-to-back will lead to a truckload of work and a limited amount of time to do it in, which in turn can implode into the one thing you always dread in the work environment—being late.

Understand That You Have Limits!

The majority of people, especially in the work environment, struggle with this reality. To be fair, many times this fault lies with the management and leadership of a business. However, when it comes to your home life, you need to be fair to yourself. You need to understand that you will always have limits, and you may not know exactly how long it will take to complete all the necessary tasks during the day. One way to understand how long it will really take to complete items on your to-do list is to time yourself. For example, I know for a fact it takes me about 25 minutes to write around 1,000 words. Idealistically, I would then think that I could complete 8,000 words in four hours. Yet this does not factor in things such as bathroom breaks, meal or snack breaks, unforeseen interruptions, and more. So in actuality, 8,000 words could end up taking me closer to six or seven hours to write. This is a much more realistic and gracious limit to place on myself.

Make Use of Technology

It seems as if we're all in a rush these days. Life has not always been like that, so why should you not use every tool and capability available to feel less rushed? One way to reduce the pressure on yourself is to turn off social media and email notifications before you start your work session (unless, of course, emails are a critical part of your job). Set yourself a timer on your phone or your watch that can let you know when the time you have set aside to work is up. You can then check in on your progress and see whether or not you are running behind in your overall agenda for the day. Remember to proactively reschedule or delegate any other items that cannot be accomplished within your current schedule.

Do NOT Multitask

This is a big no-no, especially if you do not want to negatively affect the quality of your work. People sometimes believe that because they have so much to do, they should try to accomplish as many things as they can at one time. However, most people cannot effectively multitask, no matter how appealing the idea sounds. The only time multitasking may actually save you time and effort is if you are doing a small, rote task alongside a more involved or complicated task.

Allow Yourself to Prioritize the Moment

This is an extension of multitasking. You really want to give your full attention to the task at hand, specifically for the hours that you need to work, but also for your family and self-care. You know how it feels when you are having a conversation with someone and their eyes are glued to their phone. Not only is it rude, but you know full well their concentration is not on your conversation. This can also mean that anything you ask of them will probably be forgotten by the time they need to get around to it.

If You Need to "Squeeze" It Into Your Schedule, Just Say No

If someone asks you for a favor, and you think, "Perhaps I could squeeze it in before my lunch break," let me stop you right there. This is a very good indicator that you need to say no. You can tell the person that you appreciate them thinking of you, but you are really incapable of helping at this moment and time.

Schedule Some "Me" Time

It is important that you make room in your schedule for some personal time that is blocked out for whatever you choose to do. Whenever something comes up or someone wants to fill up your "me" time, simply say no because you already have other plans. It doesn't matter if that time is going to be dedicated to taking a bubble bath, reading a book, or catching up on your favorite show, it is your time to with what you wish. Do not allow yourself to get so worn out by work and house responsibilities that you don't even have a small chunk of time alone to do something for yourself.

Other Steps to Simplify Your Daily Routines

Apart from avoiding overscheduling, there are other steps you can take to simplify your daily routines and tasks:

- Learn to work with your natural rhythms. This means you need to pay attention to and honor what is natural and feels easy for you. You might plan to do your daily clean-up in the morning but then find that doing it in the afternoon is actually relaxing.
- Build in a level of flexibility. Although this won't work for everyone, some people find flexibility to be very

important. You might find that your daily needs change, or you might just crave some variety! This means that, despite all the tasks and chores on your to-do list, you can switch up the times that you do them. Another area where you might have to build flexibility is how and when you practice self-care. For example, if you have children taking a nap, then that would be an ideal time for some self-care. If you struggle with a little bit of insomnia, then you might need to find time to add in some rest or even a nap throughout the day. It's important to understand that not every day will go as planned.

- Remember to embrace imperfection. Life happens, and things will not always go the way you expect or want them to. The moment you accept this reality, then you are one step closer to simplifying things. You might have a system up and running, but you will have the occasional diversion. That is OKAY. You can breathe and realize that these matters are not the end of the world.

I suppose this chapter is a combination of simplifying matters in your life but also a bit of a reality check. Rarely does anything go perfectly, but that should not stop you from trying and pushing forward in life. The exact same thing can be said when organizing your home.

Key Principles to Consider

- Learn to say no to favors and tasks that you have to "squeeze" into your schedule.
- Do not multitask.
- Remember to schedule some time for yourself.
- Remember to always be flexible with the unpredictability of life.

Thoughts for Reflection

- Do I say yes to everyone who asks me for a favor, even to my own detriment? Am I a "yes-man"?
- What steps can I take to start simplifying my day-to-day routine?
- What changes can I make to my schedule to open up some time for myself?

HABIT 4: USING LESS STUFF AND UTILIZING MORE SPACE

Did you know that professional organizers make an average annual salary of around $76,337 (*How to Become*, 2020)?

I never quite understood how people could make a profession out of organizing someone else's home, but as I started watching video clips of people organizing different spaces, packing and sorting items accordingly, and creating a cleaner, more beautiful space, my mind was blown—there really is an art to it!

If there is one thing from which we can learn about how to organize, it is the tiny home movement that has been taking the world by storm. People who live in so-called tiny homes live in incredibly small spaces, so every inch in the house counts. Therefore, who do you think knows best about keeping less stuff and maximizing space?

This chapter includes ideas inspired by the tiny home movement that you can consider applying in your own home.

Take a Look at Wall Space

If you don't have walls then you don't have a house, yet they are one of the most untapped space resources in a house. Think about your own home as well as those of your neighbors, friends, and family members. How many people make use of the walls by installing shelves or by using bookcases that reach the ceiling? How many hooks and other hanging apparatuses are there?

My favorite example is how a family used cupboards to divide a large room in two so that two sisters could each have their own space. Their "walls" are the very cupboards they use to store their clothes and other belongings. I thought it was brilliant and certainly do commend them for the creativity and effort that went into this unique solution.

Double Duty Is Becoming More Popular

I have to give it to people: Their creativity absolutely blows my mind. Nowadays, you can find furniture that has multiple functions. Can you think of any examples? One would be a couch that can be converted into a bed or a bed that folds up into the wall, opening up a whole lot of extra space in the room. Or how about a bench or coffee table with hidden storage compartments?

Another favorite of mine is the stairs storage tactic. Stairs take up a whole lot of space, but instead of just giving up that extra space, people have installed storage compartments within the stairs, sometimes hidden, sometimes open. Although accessing items stored there may not always be quick and easy, it is certainly a feasible option if people are running short on space.

Awkward Spaces

Instead of staring at the weird gap in one corner of the house, why not turn it into a do-it-yourself (DIY) project? Making custom shelving can be inexpensive, and you can customize the shelves to fit almost any awkward space or nook available. Making use of awkward spaces can provide extra storage and add a cool, unique aesthetic to your home.

Using Doors

Doors are meant for opening and closing, right? But you can also use doors to increase your home's storage by hanging hooks on the door in order to hang up items to keep them handy and within reach. For example, hooks can be used to hang up your bathrobe or towels. You can also hang cleaning and cooking utensils in the kitchen and handbags and jewelry in your bedroom.

Consider Investing in a Vintage Ladder

You do not actually have to invest in a specific vintage ladder; you can probably pick up one for cheap at the secondhand stores or flea markets in your area. They are perfect for extra storage or to display items and can be used for jewelry, towels, blankets, and shoes. Vintage ladders add a great design element as well as versatility for use.

Clever Ways to Best Make Use of the Space You Have

I always find myself scrounging around for more space. As more things begin to pile up and create clutter, I am left with no choice but to get creative. You will especially feel this pinch if you are downsizing, but you also want to make your home feel spacious and welcoming. The majority of us cannot afford the space that we actually need with the items that we own; however, that doesn't mean that, with a little bit of creativity, you can't create yourself a space that feels incredibly welcoming and homey.

- You can start off by opening up your entryway. Considering this is the first space in your home that your guests and you yourself see upon entering the house, the foyer in your house should both be functional, efficient, and welcoming. Don't you have space for a bench? Consider installing hooks. Hanging a large mirror can also help the space feel bigger.

- Make your kitchen functional for cooking. This might sound obvious, but at the same time, kitchens are not always designed in a functional way. If you have ever played the Sims, you know that the placement of the kitchen in their house forces them to walk back and forth through it. Although the design looks good, it gets a big "F" for practicality. The kitchen is often the busiest room in a home, as well as a commonly shared space. You and other members of your household probably spend a good amount of time there cooking, making snacks, and even helping to prepare for when you have guests coming over, so you want to focus on maximizing every bit of space with solutions such as vertical storage shelving inside of your pantry. You can even use drawer and cabinet organizers for dried, boxed, and canned goods, and food storage containers will become your best friend.

- One of the first rooms you see in the morning and one of the last you see at night can actually have some of the worst storage options. Focus on maximizing the potential of the bathroom by working out who needs to use the bathroom and when and how exactly it is used. For shared bathrooms, consider installing open shelving and using baskets that can be placed underneath the sink or on the countertop. You can also consider converting a shoe organizer into a more functional space-saver where things like accessories, brushes, combs, makeup, and other necessary products you tend to find in a bathroom can be stored.

- It seems like the living rooms and family rooms in our homes are always in need of more space. These are the rooms that often look as if a tornado recently swept through. They can be the messiest rooms in the house because they often get the most traffic. Friends come over and family spends a lot of time there, sprawling all over the couch, eating snacks, and watching TV. One way to maximize space in these rooms is to invest in multifunctional furniture. The hidden space will be such a lifesaver when you have a busy room filled with people.

- Understand that children's rooms are not just for sleeping. Depending on your child, their room should not just be for their naps but also a space for them to play and relax. Children spend a lot of time in their rooms studying, playing, and even daydreaming from time to time, so you can maximize the space they have by having functional features such as shelves, hooks, toy boxes, bulletin boards, and more. Provide them with storage solutions that keep their room clear of clutter but also give them the ability to access their belongings themselves.

- Really go all-out with making the most of your bedroom. Each bedroom should feel like a place of refuge. Make it a relaxing place to go to bed in and a place you want to see when you first wake up. Ensure that all the closet space in your house is being used as it should. Store out-of-season clothing under the bed in storage containers and invest in closet organizers that can help keep your clothes stored and organized. You really do want your closet to be functional, and utilizing the space well helps keep the rest of the room free from clutter.

- Smaller rooms and homes don't have to be a challenge to keep organized and clutter-free. Studio apartments or small homes are generally viewed as a storage nightmare, but in fact, they actually force you to prioritize what you need. A little creativity goes a long way in maximizing small spaces.

- Avoid hiding clutter or junk inside the garage. This might be very tempting, and no one in the world will blame you for considering it as an option. However, your garage was not built for the storage of items you never want to see again (because trust me, you will). Instead, maximize the space by getting rid of any unwanted furniture, broken appliances, and whatever else is no longer needed and just taking up space. Make the best use of the space you have by installing ceiling racks, shelving, and hooks for things like luggage, recreation equipment, tools, and even seasonal decorations and lawn equipment. Also, try to save some space to fit your vehicles in there, considering that is the original purpose of the garage.

- The outside of your home should be a reflection of the home you have inside. Saving space outside is not always an issue, but you want to keep your outdoor space looking neat and uncluttered as well. Consider investing in outdoor storage items such as tubs or even a shed to help keep the outside of your home looking as nice and welcoming as the inside.

Understanding Home Aesthetics

This might seem a little odd to find in a book about home management, but alongside a good organizational system, spending time developing the aesthetics in your home can really go further in making it a peaceful place free of stress where you want to spend time. It is often believed that money, success, and a great career are the keys to happiness. However, studies such as the Gallup happiness surveys show that people's happiness tends to coincide with whether or not they live in cities that are considered aesthetically beautiful.

The environment that surrounds you can contribute to your overall happiness. It is always peaceful and serene to drive down a street lined with flowering trees with sunlight glittering through the branches.

Delving further into the art and beauty of nature, we see that aesthetics really play a large and rather influential role in our day-to-day lives. Although we cannot always contribute to the appearance of the city we live in or even our general work environment, a person can certainly improve the aesthetic sensibility in their own home.

Improving the aesthetics in your home will open the door for us to appreciate the beauty in our everyday lives. The following sections provide some tips to help develop the aesthetics in your home.

The Importance of Design in the Home Aesthetic

A part of me has always wondered why I enjoyed visiting some homes more than others. I mean, they all have the same things: bedrooms, bathrooms, living rooms, a kitchen. Yet there is no denying that some houses held a greater appeal for me. For one, I can think about when I visited a vacation home down at the beach. I remember the bright white walls, beach-themed furniture and decor, and the cozy bedrooms. One bedroom had a blue theme with dolphin accents while the other had a sea-green motif. I fell in love with the house all because of its aesthetics.

The one prominent factor that plays a role in home aesthetics is design. It is the most basic concept, and you will want to break down the interior design into different categories. Naturally, the colors you choose for your bathroom may greatly vary from the colors you choose for your kitchen.

The aesthetics can really have an impact on your overall mood. Different colors are known to evoke different sorts of feelings. For instance, you may associate the color blue with calm, green with vigor, red with energy, and so forth. So when you choose the colors within your house, they will play a small role in your feelings and moods. Vibrant colors tend to evoke feelings of energy whereas warm colors help to communicate a welcoming coziness, and cooler colors can give off calm, serene vibes.

The aesthetics of your home are one of the best ways to show off your personality. From the furniture down to the cutlery, having the creativity to be yourself and to enjoy your surroundings (and have others enjoy them as well) are benefits of putting thought and effort into your home's aesthetics.

What Is Modern and What is Traditional?

First, you'll want to determine if your personal style is more modern or traditional when you think about the aesthetics you want for your house. You can consider timeless as well as classic interior designs, or you can focus on the more minimalist and functional designs that have arisen in this modern era.

- Traditional: This is a style that focuses primarily on forms of carved woodwork and modeling. Much of the furniture is sturdy and was created with the influence of the 18th and 19th centuries. This furniture tends to incorporate lots of detail and elegance.
- Modern: This is a stark contrast to a traditional aesthetic. Often you can find this style in hotels and tech businesses. This kind of design really focuses on the minimalist aesthetic. The architectural lines tend to be clean, and the space has an open feel. The modern aesthetic focuses more on what is practical and functional. Think about it this way: Whenever you see a heavy oak wood desk with carvings on the edges, it is elegant and beautiful but moving it is a nightmare. On the flip side, if you have a smaller desk that is adjustable and has moveable shelving at the bottom and lockable wheels, it has a very

minimalistic look to it and is much easier to move.

- Transitional: For anyone who would like to bring a little bit of both worlds into their home, this is called transitional interior design. There is a lot of creative freedom that comes with decorating the inside of your home, so feel free to get creative and combine your favorite aspects of both styles.

Color Scheme

This might not be as feasible if you are renting your home, but color schemes do not just apply to the color of the walls. Choosing complementary colors to feature in a room can make a world of difference when it comes to the overall aesthetics.

Start off with picking colors you love. This is the time when your favorite color can get whipped out, used, and abused. Once you have settled on using a color that you love, you can choose a color palette and create a color scheme that works together. You do not have to pick a traditional scheme or fit within any specific style. If you can, and you want to, paint the walls with the colors you like—it will give the house a very satisfying visual appeal. If painting is not an option for you, then you can make up for it with your pieces of furniture and other decors.

You can make use of color theory in order to choose specific color combinations that will work well. If your favorite color is, for instance, pink, consider mixing in other colors to use with it—unless, of course, you want your house to look like Barbie's dreamhouse. For instance, gray goes very well with pink. You can also use other colors to enhance a specific color in the combination. For example, red and green are excellent colors when used together, and yellow and blue are also good complementary color choices.

Space and Areas You Want to Use

It's a good idea to consider furniture that revolves around and enhances your lifestyle. For instance, if you live by the minimalist ideology, then you might want to focus on furniture that had been created with industrial-looking materials and is more compact. If you have a little more space, then you can consider getting larger sets of furniture. A good example of this is your dining table. People tend to choose their dining table depending on the size and space you have in their eating area.

Furniture Aesthetics

Another rule of thumb is to choose furniture colors that fit into your color scheme. Wood is a good addition that works well with warm colors, and plastic and metal go well with blue and white color schemes. More elaborate furniture normally works well with yellows and browns.

Aesthetics

You want to have a solid idea of what aesthetic you are going for when picking out your furniture. Plastic and metal are ideal if you want to go for a modern look, and classic and vintage tend to look good with bronze, teak wood, or fabric-based pieces.

So now you have learned the basics of incorporating intentional aesthetics into your home. Again, this is simply a possible addition to your home's appearance. You might not have the budget or the capability of enhancing your home's aesthetics right now, but as time progresses, you might find yourself slowly sliding into a theme of your choosing. It will make a world of difference in the long run.

Key Principles to Consider

- Everything you place in your house needs to have some form or function whether it be decorative, for storage, or multi-purpose.
- There is a science to color affecting your overall mood.
- Appealing aesthetics in your home can create a more organized appearance.

Thoughts for Reflection

- What items in your home take up too much space? Can you replace them with furniture that is more functional?
- How does the overall theme of your house impact your mood?
- How can you incorporate your style preferences into your home?
- How can you use aesthetics to help improve organization?

HABIT 5: FOLLOWING THE ONE-MINUTE RULE

One thing I know about myself is that deadlines are my strongest ally and worst enemy. I recall time and again scrambling left and right to make sure a task is done in the designated amount of time, and after heavy bouts of stress, I always seem to manage. However, I knew that one day, this nasty habit of mine would lead me into a whole load of trouble. It eventually did when my own family members started complaining about my bad habits. I knew something needed to change.

I started small by making sure that I took care of the little tasks when they first came up. Slowly I progressed to bigger tasks and finally reached a point where I no longer have to stress about getting everything done in time.

Procrastination is one of the most formidable enemies people will ever come face-to-face with, especially those who have to deal with endless deadlines and projects. Procrastination can sneak in when you least expect it to and causes chaos and stress wherever it goes.

Why Is Procrastination So Harmful?

We all joke about procrastination, and some even go so far as to brag about it as if it is a skill. We all can relate to the problem of delaying projects until the last minute, which in turn can cause sleepless nights and extra stress, not to mention it keeps us stuck at our desks until the task is actually completed.

What does procrastination actually look like? To put it very simply, procrastination is putting off a task that seems tedious or unpleasant. That means you can be busy and still be procrastinating because you are avoiding the tasks that actually need doing with tasks that seem easier or more fun.

One common procrastination trick is when people decide to miraculously clean their room the moment they need to study or focus on a very boring project. Why? Well, the cleaning needs to be done anyway and somehow seems more interesting than actually having to sit down and grind in comparison.

In short, procrastination is the enemy of our happiness, productivity, and health. It seeps in to attack our companies and communities.

Who would have thought that the "I'll do it later" mentality could actually pose such an enormous threat?

Common Traits of a Procrastinator

People waste an average of 218 minutes on a daily basis, which is the equivalent of wasting 55 days in a year (Atik, 2015). This is a jarring statistic to say the least.

How can we determine whether or not we are chronic procrastinators? By examining our habits, of course. After all, procrastination tends to lead to very similar tendencies, even though we do not altogether want to admit this.

As a norm, procrastinators want to avoid revealing the information they have in regard to their abilities. They tend to make assumptions about how much time they have that are generally poor, and they tend to dwell a whole lot more on the past.

Procrastinators also do not act on their intentions, might portray perfectionist characteristics, do not have a lot of competitiveness in them, lack self-control, suffer from depression and anxiety, and participate in self-deceit. These might seem all a little extreme, but in reality, procrastination really has a very ugly side to it.

Why Do People Procrastinate?

Why do people delay tasks to the last minute? Why do I often find myself scrambling for my phone upon realizing that the due date is imminent?

We have all participated in some form of procrastination from time to time. If it happens on occasion, it is generally not the end of the world, but it turns into a problem if it becomes a habit. Habits are difficult to break.

There are many reasons people procrastinate. For some, it could be a form of rebellion, and maybe others were never taught the skills to manage their time more effectively and take the initiative on tasks or projects. Some people may even find they are scared to begin a task because their tendency for perfectionism makes them fear messing up, and still others procrastinate simply due to pure boredom.

It is incredibly easy to get distracted in this day and age. Social media and technology have crippled some people's ability to pay proper attention. TikTok, a social media app compiled of short video clips, is a great example of how social media can keep us from accomplishing goals or working on projects. Watching short videos one after another can be addicting, and before you know it, you've wasted hours watching TikTok videos.

How Do People Procrastinate?

There are generally two types of procrastination.

One is called "behavioral procrastination." This is where people shift the blame and avoid taking action. It is considered a form of self-sabotage and can really hinder a person's overall goals and dreams. People who struggle with this form of procrastination often struggle with lower levels of self-esteem and have a lot of doubt about themselves and what they can accomplish. They think that if they never finish a task, no one will be able to judge their ability —and this can apply even to the very corners of one's home.

This form of procrastination can be prolonged, which in turn can lead to a cycle of self-defeating behavior. It works like a downward spiral, and people who are caught up in it can really struggle to get themselves out of it.

The other form of procrastination is called "decisional procrastination." This is where someone puts off the need to make a decision when faced with certain choices or conflicts.

People who engage in a lot of decisional procrastination find themselves to be very scared of making mistakes, and they are more likely to be perfectionists. Procrastinators will start looking for more information or possible alternatives when it comes to making a choice.

However, being overinformed can often lead to even more self-sabotage due to having created so many choices for themselves that they are now trapped in optional paralysis because they want to make sure they make the right decision—the problem is, which one of the vast array of dizzying options is the "right" one?

How Do You Overcome Procrastination?

Procrastination involves many elements, and there is no easy answer. Procrastination is not about time management, and telling yourself or someone who is struggling to just "do it" is not going to be a magical cure either. We are all human, not a Nike commercial.

However, there is one strategy that has been commonly and successfully adopted by people struggling with procrastination: the one-minute rule.

One-Minute Rule

A friend of mine always had a problem with getting things done on time. Even the smallest of tasks might get delayed by days or even weeks. She kept getting into trouble at work, and her house was a mess.

That is until she learned the one-minute rule. Did she need to file some paperwork? The one-minute rule compelled her to take the paper, get out of her chair, and place it in the filing cabinet. In the end, it took all of 30 seconds.

She began responding to texts from her boss almost immediately, and her coworkers noticed that she became increasingly reliable as time went on. And small tasks that would once have been put off for days began to only take about a minute each before she carried on with her other tasks.

Can one little rule solve your procrastination problem? Well, yes and no. Yes, it can introduce to you a brand new system to help your procrastination, but without the proper motivation to defeat procrastination, then no. This rule by itself can only take you so far.

So let's dive into what the one-minute rule is. It is a very handy strategy for someone who is overwhelmed by the piled-up laundry and a growing to-do list. You may find yourself having to write down all the different appointments and tasks, keeping yourself a nice binder or list on your phone, but you might have an issue with the small and tedious tasks in your home. This is one rule you can embrace to help make your life, and perhaps the lives of your family members, a whole lot easier.

The rule is this: If you come across a task that will take you one minute or less to complete, do it the moment you realize that it has to be done.

Tedious but small tasks make this rule quite easy to follow. Suddenly, you are not spending too much time jotting on your notepad all the tasks that need to be done. Rather, all the small tasks are under control and dealt with promptly.

If you can commit to following this one rule, it can bring you one step closer to feeling much less overwhelmed—and it can help you to become far more organized in a matter of literal seconds.

Why Does the One-Minute Rule Work?

I often think of the times when people ask me for favors. If they ask me for a favor that can take me a good five or ten minutes, I tend to struggle. However, if they come to me with a task that takes around 30 seconds, suddenly it is something I am far more willing to do.

We all value our time, and the one-minute rule is helpful to those who just need to get a better grip on their time and for people who tend to put off specific things.

A good example of where this rule could be applicable is in the kitchen. How long would it take to clean a dirty dish? It might take you 30, maybe 45 seconds, especially if you clean it right after you have eaten off it.

Imagine if everyone in the household cleaned a dirty dish right after they used it and perhaps even threw in an extra pot or two. The kitchen would suddenly be much neater on a consistent basis, and it only took a single minute of a person's time.

However, if you are a chronic procrastinator, the one-minute rule might take more effort to implement as a habit, but what is stopping you from giving it a go?

What are some of the major areas in which the one-minute rule can help?

- Housework: It is all too easy to just let the household chores pile up like those clothes on the chair. It is so easy to leave socks on the floor, a coffee mug on the dining room table, or the screwdriver on the porch. Then the state of the house gradually grows worse and worse, which can lead to a point of great frustration and stress. Once you apply the one-minute rule, all these "pile-ups" will slowly start disappearing, and you as a family can certainly rejoice when you see that happen.
- Email and communication: I tend to find myself reading and not responding to messages more often than I'd like to admit, which then leads to the awkward "Sorry I haven't responded" text a week

after the original message was sent. Learning to respond using the one-minute rule will save you time—and awkwardness—when it comes to matters of communication.

The one-minute rule can really build on someone's sense of accomplishment. Suddenly, you see tasks and chores getting done and fewer things piling up. However, when it comes to chronic procrastination, what are some other things you can do to help overcome this?

Overcoming Chronic Procrastination

Although you will certainly benefit from the one-minute rule, it can't solve all your procrastination problems, so you may want to add some extra steps to your routine. Procrastination tends to show itself very prominently in a person's home, so the efficiency, cleanliness, and organization of a person's living space suffer the most from the bad habits of procrastination.

- Figure out why you are procrastinating. Finding the reason can lead you to the right answer. For example, you might find it hard to be motivated until the deadline is looming ever closer, feeling that you "work best under pressure." You might struggle with difficult, negative thoughts, or maybe you find the task boring or overwhelming.

- If you have a very large task, such as reorganizing your entire house, break it down into small steps; you can even see if you can find a way to fit in the one-minute rule. You want to make sure the tasks are doable within the amount of time you have. A huge project can feel like a hike up a steep mountain, but when you break it down for yourself, you are shrinking the mountain (if only it could work that way in real hikes). If you really struggle to visualize or break it down, you can always ask a friend you trust to help you think things through and organize the steps.
- Set deadlines for yourself. Once you have the tasks broken down into various smaller parts, create deadlines for each of those smaller parts. That way, you can enjoy the success of completing the short-term goals while making good and steady progress to your long-term goals.

- Make use of positive peer pressure. Having someone to check up on you and your progress is a fantastic way of helping you stick to your goals and keep you moving. Self-motivation might not always be enough, but whenever it comes to encouragement from our peers, it can be easier to feel motivated. Peer pressure can have a very positive effect on people if used the right way.
- Alternate between different tasks. Another way to keep your interest level and motivation peaked is to focus on two tasks during the same time period. You can set a timer that you will use to switch between the two tasks. This is a classic way that you can make boring tasks more interesting simply because you have added in some variety.
- Cut off the distractions. It could be anything, but the likely biggest guilty party is your smartphone. Steer clear of anything else that distracts you from starting or finishing your task.
- Understand that you can be busy but also still be procrastinating. You may feel like you are very busy, but if you do not

finish your high-priority tasks first, you are still struggling with procrastination.

- Delegation isn't illegal. Sometimes you need to learn the difference between procrastinating and simply not having the time. I have, time and again, blamed myself for not completing a task while forgetting all the matters and circumstances around me that made completing that task more difficult.
- Do not allow negative thoughts to control you. Negative thoughts can cause a downward spiral and defeat you before the battle even begins. In fact, thoughts and feelings are incredibly powerful, and once you learn to talk to yourself in a way that is positive and gentle, you might find it a whole lot easier to take the necessary action.

Remember, you are not going to overcome procrastination right away! It is a process, and all processes take time. Adopting the one-minute rule for your household is certainly a good place to start and might even trigger a domino effect of radical changes over time.

After all, it is a simple rule with practical applications and positive outcomes.

Key Principles to Consider

- Procrastination is harmful in many aspects but will especially hinder the success of organizing your home.
- Focus on cutting off distractions that contribute to your procrastination.
- The one-minute rule can help you tackle small tasks immediately.
- There are steps you can take to overcome procrastination on larger tasks.

Thoughts for Reflection

- How often do you procrastinate?
- Does procrastination hinder your ability to complete important tasks?
- How does procrastination affect your home in general?
- How can you start applying the one-minute rule in your life?

HABIT 6: DESIGNATE A PLACE FOR EVERYTHING IN YOUR HOME

Imagine this: You always lose your pens in your workspace, and you never seem to know where they end up. All you do know is that your family members are in the habit of borrowing your pens. But how often do they bring them back?

A solution to this problem could be for you to make a new rule and tell your family that if a borrowed pen is not returned within an hour, you will never lend your pen to that person again.

Suddenly all your pens start appearing again, and you no longer have to revisit the office supply store.

You should focus on having a designated place for everything in your home. This does not necessarily mean you have to obsessively file and label everything (although labeling is great, and we'll talk more about it later in this book), but it does mean that you designate certain spaces for certain items and practice the habit of always putting them there. When you have a family involved, get them on board with this, too. Otherwise, you'll continue to face a world of frustration when others don't put things back where they belong.

This section contains tips on how to find the right places for objects in your home.

Place the Like Things With the Like Things

Okay, this might sound a little confusing, but hear me out. Your organizational skills will increase greatly once you place similar things together. You want to place everything in your house in certain categories. For example, jeans will be in one drawer or section of your closet, coffee mugs will be on the top shelf of the cupboard, your wine glasses will be stored in their own space, and your pens are always at your desk. Once you see how many similar things you do have, you may also decide to clear out any extra items you no longer use or need.

Taking an Inventory

Being a professional organizer is a real career, and one thing they do is take inventory. You don't know what you have and what you do not need until you have it all written down. It might seem strange since it's not like you're running a shop in your own home, but there is a reason why shops are so effective with their organization. Everything has a place, and they constantly keep stock of what they have and what they need to get. You simply need to take this principle and apply it in your very own home. It can aid in the decluttering process because it allows you to "edit" your possessions. For example, any clothing you have not worn for over 12 months can be donated, and bathroom or kitchen products that might have expired can be thrown out, as can anything that has not served you well over the last year. Items that are in good condition and can still be used can be given away or sold; items that are no longer usable should be discarded.

Check Out Your Space Before You Start Organizing

You want to understand what you are working with before you designate spots for your various items. You want to analyze your space and make a plan on how you want to use it. For instance, you probably won't want to place your soap products right next to the spice rack, you will want your stationery separate from your winter coats, and so on. So you want to plan just exactly how much space you need and what you want to use it for. There is a general level of common sense that goes into deciding what you put where.

You also want to make sure your space and organization will also match the aesthetic that you have going. The aesthetic might not be as important, but it can radically affect the overall appearance of your home. In general, it helps keep things consistent if you try working within the theme you've already established. Appearances do make a difference in the feel of your home.

Put a Label on Everything

Once you have gone through and sorted all the day's organization projects, it might be handy to start labeling. Think of this as the cherry on top of your organization sundae. It can make your organizational system more sustainable by reminding everyone in your household where everything goes. So, although labeling isn't altogether necessary, it can be very handy if you are not living alone and you need to guide people on their journey with you.

Tackle One Space at a Time

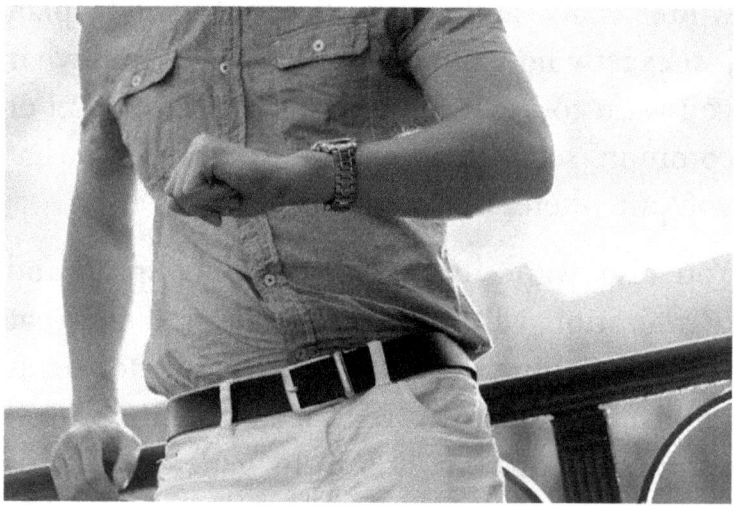

We all love radical transformations on TV, but in reality, huge sweeping changes in a matter of days are not always feasible. In addition to making changes in your life, you have to deal with work, your partner, and your kids, plus remembering to eat and shower from time to time. Next thing you know, most of your time has been swallowed up. Organizing can also be a very stress-filled activity, and the majority of experts recommend that you start small. It can help the project feel perhaps a little less daunting by starting at point A and moving on to point B. You need to make a commitment to schedule time to organize in your daily schedule, but be realistic about how much time you have to spend on it each day.

The best place to start is to choose the place that is used most frequently in your house. This will naturally have the biggest impact on your day-to-day life and help give you the confidence you need to move on to the other matters on your list. Once you have chosen the space where you will begin your organizational journey, take everything out, sort through it, and see what exactly you want to keep and what you can get rid of.

Set Aside Time for Each Project

You will never be able to organize anything unless you carve out time specifically for each project in your schedule. Some projects will take longer than others, so don't rush a project that you know needs more time.

Also, try to apply the "one in and the one out" rule every time you buy something. Shopping can be a fun and relaxing activity, but try to avoid overfilling the spaces that you are trying to keep organized and consider adopting a system in which you donate, sell, or throw away an item you no longer need or use each time you bring a new item into the house. This can help prevent an overflow of possessions that can turn into clutter.

Key Principles to Consider

- Everything you use should always be put back where it belongs.
- Get your family on board with your organizational rules.
- When organizing a larger area, start with one smaller area and only move on to the next once your work in the original spot is completed.
- Schedule time for organizing.

Thoughts for Reflection

- How many items are in your home that you do not actually need?
- How much time have you spent organizing a single area in the house?
- Do you put things back where they belong?

HABIT 7: PLACE ITEMS IN YOUR HOME WHERE THEY WILL BE USED ACCORDINGLY

In this chapter, we'll be talking about some useful storage tips. It might seem kind of obvious to not place a pen in the bathroom or to not have your spaghetti stored in the linen closet, but storing items effectively might not be as easy as you might think either. You have your basic items, such as clothes, bathroom products, and food, which have obvious places in your home. But where exactly in the kitchen should you place the spices for instance?

What do you do with the clean towels? Where do you store the extra toilet paper?

Suddenly it is not so easy figuring out a place for everything, especially if your home is limited in space. The main principle and habit should be to place the items in your home where they will be used accordingly. The following sections will help you determine where and how to store certain items.

Ways to Store at Home

It's important to understand that there should be a place for everything. A messy home is often not caused by laziness but simply because people may be unsure of where they should put their things.

To be fair, many houses are not necessarily built with storage in mind, so it is up to you to adapt your home for optimal storage. Soon you might discover little tips and tricks can really go a long way in maximizing storage space.

For one, consider learning how to fold things in a compact way; this can create more space in your dresser drawers and closet. When you make your closet tidy, you are opening up space elsewhere for other things, so learning the art of effective folding should probably be on your to-do list.

You may also want to consider using dividers in your dresser drawers and closet shelves to create more order among the items and make things easier to find. Dividers are often cheap, and you can find ones that fit your cupboards and overall aesthetics.

When you use dividers, you can store things according to their size and purpose. That means you will waste less time when trying to find things you need. Throw in some labeling to sweeten the pot.

Kitchen Storage

Did you know that equipment meant for the office can actually be very useful in the kitchen? CD organizers can double as a rack to store your pots and pans. Just because CDs and DVDs are slowly going extinct doesn't mean you have to get rid of their storage devices! Instead, recycle them in the kitchen.

Another idea for the kitchen is to make use of hangers, magnets, and clips for your utensils. Having your knives, whisks, pots, and pans all hanging up on hooks can make the kitchen organized and efficient because, instead of rummaging through drawers looking for what you need, it becomes a simple matter of grabbing the item and carrying on.

Consider installing some additional shelves to make more space for dishes, glasses, and mugs in the cupboard, or you can consider placing an extra shelf over your cupboards in order to create more space. You want to avoid allowing stacks of dishes to become top-heavy and straining the rack or shelf they are placed on. If you have more shelves, you have more space to keep stacks of dishes shorter and less likely to topple.

Anything that you rarely use should be stored out of the way. The last thing you want is to use up good, useful storage space with items you use only once a year. This is the same reason storing holiday decor in the garage is a good option.

For items such as aluminum foil, plastic wrap, and storage bags, a vertical paper holder is a very cool idea. A wall shelf is excellent for storing your recipe books, and you can save space in your drawers and on your counters by having the dish drainer attached to a wall right above the kitchen sink.

You can store your knives and other metallic utensils using a strong magnetic strip mounted on the wall. This can also work for your spices if the containers or lids are metal.

Hand utensils such as silverware generally work well being stored in a drawer, and you can find handy utensil organizing trays. Paper holders are excellent for storing water bottles, and in smaller kitchens, you can consider having a folding table installed.

Finally, consider using vertical shelves for storing cutting boards, baking pans, and other upright items. This makes them easy to store as well as easy to grab.

Bathroom Storage

So what can you do with bathroom storage? Here are a few useful ideas to consider:

- Brighten the same by having reflected light by installing a mirrored cabinet. If you have a small bathroom, this is especially ideal. You can use it to store small items, and some cabinets have internal compartments that can really be helpful for storing things like tweezers, toothbrush, toothpaste, and so on.
- Avoid using oversized storage items. Bathroom sizes certainly vary, and you want to create a space that is both sleek and neat. It might be tempting to hide everything in hidden storage, but you do

not necessarily have to shut everything away, so try to find storage solutions that fit the size of your bathroom.

- Look for storage items with deep but narrow drawers and shelves because they will allow you to separate everything into different compartments. For instance, you want your hairbrush and other hair accessories together, but you do not want them mixed in with your lotions and shampoo.
- Investing in a vanity unit may well be worth your while. Considering most of us spend a good amount of time getting ready every day, vanities allow for a variety of storage options, and they look great, too!
- If space allows it in your bathroom, consider adding a central island which can create plenty of storage space for toiletries, towels, and more.
- Consider investing in customized cupboards for the bathroom, especially if there are none already. Decorative cupboards not only add to the atmosphere but are excellent storage options.

- Remember that you have a lot of creative freedom when it comes to your bathroom storage!

Storage Rules to Follow

Rules can occasionally be a little overwhelming, yet a person cannot ignore the fact that an efficient rule can turn the household into an effective and organized space. Here are some rules meant to help optimize your storage and organization:

- Consider choosing square storage containers. Unless you have an open-shelving space, square containers are one of the best options for maximizing your space. Round containers don't fit as snugly against the wall or in a corner.
- Invest in quality containers, especially if you are storing clothes in a closet. It might be tempting to go for cardboard boxes, but eventually, they wear out, break, and sometimes bugs and mice can get in, damaging the goods.
- Always be on the lookout for "nesters." Nesters, as the name suggests, are

containers that have the same shape but graduated sizes and can "nest" into one another when stacked.
- Think about the variety of containers you buy. Sets with multiple containers often only have one container of each size, so think about what you need to store and the best-sized container for each type of item.
- Take note of the amount of storage space you have. If you notice you don't have enough space for all of your storage containers until after you've started boxing everything up, you are working backward, not forward.

Storage Rules for Small Spaces

We all have spent time in our lives in limited spaces. However, if you ever find yourself living in a cramped space, here are some handy storage tips to follow:

- Tip 1: Double-duty furniture. Every time you buy yourself a piece of furniture, consider a piece that has storage options. It can be a bed with hidden compartments or a coffee table with drawers. There is no rule that your furniture can't both look nice and offer useful functions.

- Tip 2: Look up. There is a lot of potential for storage within the vertical space of your home. Things like floating or tall shelving can really make use of what would otherwise be wasted space.

- Tip 3: Sleep on it. The area right underneath your bed is a great resource for storage space for items such as your off-season clothes, linens, or extra blankets. There are many affordable and practical under-bed storage options. Vacuum-sealed storage bags can help you open up even more space.

- Tip 4: Move it. Storage items that are movable are one of the great ways to keep items at hand yet tucked away when you need a little extra storage space. Bar carts are a truly creative way for people to keep things they use at hand when needed, and they can also be easily moved when they're not being used. For example, if you have a hobby that includes many small pieces, like beading and jewelry-

making, then it's really useful to have a single place to keep all of your supplies. When you have guests or need more space, you can keep your items organized and just push the cart out of the way.
- Tip 5: Packable storage. This tip is especially helpful for someone who frequently moves from place to place and sometimes finds themselves in rooms with insufficient storage space. You can invest in storage that can be packed up alongside all your other items and easily taken with you when you move.

*Bonus tip: Next time you're looking for a new home, be sure to take extra note of the amount of storage space in the homes you see. This is an easy aspect to overlook with the myriad of things on your mind when house-hunting.

Key Principles to Consider

- It is better to stick with simpler storage solutions in the bathroom.
- Moveable storage containers are fantastic for items you regularly use.
- It is important to pick the right storage for the right rooms.

Thoughts for Reflection

- What room in your house would you say is the least organized?
- Which room in your house would you rank as the most organized?
- Are there items in each room that don't really belong there?

HABIT 8: AVOID CREATING CLUTTER-COLLECTING AREAS

I know for a fact that my wardrobe is nearing its limits. I have spent a lot of time shoving T-shirts and socks out of the way trying to find more room in the mangled mess. It's even at the point where the door cannot close properly, but I've never thought of the contents of my wardrobe as "clutter" until I started to dig a little deeper about getting organized.

Clutter is perhaps the number one enemy that pops up like weeds in the household. How does this happen? Why does it happen? How can you identify it? Clutter can make a person feel as if the house is out of control. You might even be worried that there is something wrong with you or how you are running your household.

But we are all human. There are plenty of reasons why clutter can occur in our homes. Once you understand how clutter starts, the solutions become easier to apply. This section outlines some of the reasons you might have clutter in your home.

Problem 1

You might just simply have too much stuff. This might seem like an obvious answer. However, it is often the one people tend to struggle the most with. We often find that our closets are overflowing with clothes, yet we can't find anything to wear. We can never find tools like a screwdriver in the moments that we need them which means that we buy another one next time we're at the store, only to add more clutter to our homes!

What is the best way to solve the problem? The answer is quite simple. You need to eliminate what you don't need. The answer may be a simple one, but it's not necessarily an easy one.

Too much stuff will always create more clutter, but learning to let go of possessions can be a tough project largely because it requires you to think things through as to what you need and what you don't.

Sentimentality can also play role in struggling to let go of items. A good rule of thumb to follow when decluttering is: If you have not used it for a year or more, then it is something you can probably let go of.

What are some of the items you can immediately consider getting rid of?

- old newspaper and magazines
- more than two sets of extra bed linens per bed in the house
- any extra cooking utensils or appliances you do not use
- expired toiletries, medicines, cosmetics, and nail polish
- broken items that you haven't needed since they broke

- old technology such as CDs, DVDs, and VHS tapes

Problem 2

You may be experiencing a big transition in your life such as changing jobs, moving, having a baby, or having financial difficulties. There is always going to be something that is disruptive to your life, and we often let things pile up when we are trying to adjust to big changes.

For me, my desk space and living room start to fall into chaos whenever I embark on long projects and am working toward a deadline. Everything else I need to accomplish gets tossed to the wind, and I am left scrambling to pick up the pieces afterward, including a whole lot of clutter.

So how can you work on solving this problem? Well, you can start by focusing on the small tasks in your life and implementing the one-minute rule to help keep clutter at bay. It is unwise and impractical to wait for the ideal circumstances to come that will allow you time to focus on cleaning up. Life will always knock you about with changes, and all you can do is add the padding to make sure you don't come out too bruised on the other side.

Start off with the areas that frustrate you the most and spend just a couple of minutes a day decluttering and organizing them. A mere 15 minutes a day can go far when you focus on sorting out different matters, and keeping the house neat and efficient afterward should not be too much of a challenge.

Problem 3

Another very common problem is that you do not have an organizational system to work with. The quickest way for things to become disorganized is not having a system up and running. After all, setting everything up will take a good amount of time and effort, especially because many of us work and have relationships with family members and friends we'd like to maintain. If you do not have an organizational system in place, certain spots in the house will become magnets for clutter.

As soon as you identify that spot, you should address it at once. If you catch yourself walking toward a clutter pile with yet another load of stuff, ask yourself why you are not simply putting the stuff away. Maybe you have a bunch of bills that are piling up on that coffee table because you do not have a system for paying the bills or a proper recycling system for discarding the leftover envelopes and paper after the bills are paid. Maybe your children are in the habit of throwing their socks on the bathroom floor or their bags on the living room couch because they don't have designated places to put their items. Another common source of clutter is dishes becoming piled up on the countertops because there's no established system for loading them into the dishwasher.

If any of these scenarios sound familiar, you need to apply the system of having a designated spot for everything. You will also find it incredibly useful to label all the items in your house. Once you have a good system in place like the ones taught throughout this book, then you will certainly notice a decrease in the amount of clutter around your home.

Problem 4

You are a perfectionist. Now that might stump you; it stumped me when I first learned this. How on earth is it possible for a perfectionist to allow clutter to build up? Whether you are a perfectionist or know someone else who is, it is one thing that just doesn't seem to make sense. However, perfectionism, as much as it pushes you to go above and beyond in many aspects of your life, can also cripple a person. When you have to deal with clutter as a perfectionist, you may not feel up to the task, or you may feel like your organization system is too flawed. While this sense of getting everything 100% right is in the foreground, the clutter keeps growing in the background.

So how on earth do you unhook yourself from perfectionistic paralysis and focus on learning how to get through the rut? Well, you have to keep reminding yourself that being "perfect" is an impossible achievement and that your system doesn't have to be perfect; all it needs is to be better than it was when you started. You might not have the time to deep clean your room, never mind the entire house, so allow yourself to start by spending 15 minutes a day working on one small area in the house. Your main goal is to get it looking better than it did in the first place.

More Tips for Avoiding Clutter

Now you can identify the most common reason why you might be allowing clutter to pile up, and you have a certain strategy in mind for each. However, there are other tips and tricks you can use to avoid causing clutter in the first place.

After all, clutter is only a problem if you allow items to pile up. Right?

- Start off with committing to yourself and to your family that you will donate, recycle, or toss items that are no longer used, needed, or wanted. This might be tough at first, especially if you are not in the habit of "wasting" items, but this can actually contribute to clutter. You might feel that you will need an item in the future or that it is still useful and therefore does not deserve to be discarded despite the fact that it will go right back to the same spot and never be used. I remember when I was younger, I was a notorious "pack rat." I collected all sorts of items with the idea that I would use them in the future. However, as I grew older, the items in my room started to overwhelm me. I grabbed a bag and ruthlessly started chucking the items I had never used. To this day, I do not know what all those items were, and I certainly don't miss them. The odds of you missing any particular item that you don't use are incredibly small.

- Set a timer for yourself in order to work in short but concentrated bursts. You want to really give it your full focus in the time that you are working on a task or project. This hack is often called the "Pomodoro technique."
- Deal with decluttering as a team. If you live with your family, make everyone responsible for decluttering their own rooms. When it comes to communal spaces, people should work together to see what they want to keep and what

they want to get rid of. This way, you can unload a good chunk of the burden off yourself and focus on your section.

- Always limit the time that you are willing to store an item for someone else. This might seem a little harsh, but remember that people are using up your space, which in turn can really build the clutter. I recall all too well how many times I have had to deal with piles of clothes left by other people. Even something as simple as a box can take up valuable space. Every space in the house matters, so having a ground rule like this will prod people to remember their commitment to helping you reduce clutter.

Tricks for Staying More Organized

- Make conscious decisions about where all items should go and make sure they stay there.
- Set a limit for how many items are allowed in the house and where they can be kept.

- For each item that comes into your home, consider taking one item out.
- Create designated spaces for items that get used frequently.
- Create for yourself an action folder in order to help you clear up all the workspaces, making pending projects easy to find.
- Whenever you have to deal with paper, deal with it immediately. It can be surprising—as well as a nightmare—how quickly papers can turn into a whole tangled mess of clutter. It is not a matter of simply tossing the papers as you need to sort through them to decide what needs to be kept.
- If you really struggle with clutter, consider reaching out to friends or even self-help groups such as Clutterers Anonymous or Messies Anonymous.
- Be aware of digital clutter as well. You can minimize your digital clutter by sorting and clearing your emails regularly and making sure you place files in the right folder, and don't allow them to just drop in the downloads file without

sorting them (I am guilty as charged when it comes to this).

Top Cleaning Tips

Don't worry—I am not going to leave you in the dark when it comes to clearing the clutter and cleaning! Generally, after you shuffle around items and begin to organize them, you are going to also be cleaning the space around them. Here are some tips to help you clean:

- Make sure all the sponges and cloths are disinfected before you use them each day. You can clean them in hot soapy water, wring them out, and then soak them in disinfectant for 15 minutes. Wring them out once again and let them dry properly. There are some sponges and cloths that can be washed in the washing machine, but you will want to wash them in a hot-water cycle to make sure they are being properly disinfected.
- If you find that your vacuum cleaner has lost some suction power, you can clean it by unhooking the hose and checking the entrance of the dust bag or dust cylinder for debris that might be clogging up the

machine. Wash away the dirt properly and cut through hair or threads when cleaning out the bristles (pulling on them can damage your vacuum).

- If you want to clean your oven without chemicals, heat it up to 400° F. Place an oven-safe bowl filled with water inside and leave it in for 45 minutes. Once the oven has cooled, you can then wipe away dirt and grime with a clean cloth.
- If you want great results when you mop, consider getting a top mop. You do not have to squeeze out excess water by hand, and it works like a dream. A good rule of thumb is to use warm water to mop hard floors but not boiling water as it can cause damage.
- If you find a fingerprint on stainless steel, you can dab it away with a little bit of baby oil or simply wipe it with a clean cloth.
- Understand that baking soda's usefulness extends far beyond cooking; it is a cleaning celebrity. It deodorizes naturally and has a gentle abrasive nature.
- In order to tackle grimy grout, you have come face-to-face with. Use a mixture of

baking soda, white vinegar, and water, then rub it on the grout with an old toothbrush to scrub off the grime. A great way to save you a whole lot of elbow grease is to use an old electric toothbrush.

- One way to keep your cutting boards hygienic is to rub lemon juice on them and let them sit overnight. The next day, you can rinse them off and let them dry. If the cutting board is dishwasher safe, simply pop it in there.
- One of the best ways to keep dirt out of the house is to place a good dirt-trapping doormat at your front door. You will want to give it a good thwack outside on a weekly basis to get rid of the dirt that has collected on it. Some are even machine washable, but you will want to check whether or not your machine can handle it as certain mats can be heavy when wet.
- Always remember to use cold water while working with bleach; warm water can make the bleach ineffective and useless.
- Consider getting a couple of microfiber cloths. They are perfect for removing

dust, grime, smudges, and grease without chemicals. They are also perfect for cleaning glass.
- Recycle old socks by getting them damp and using them to clean your Venetian blinds.

Now you know the first few steps of dealing with clutter as well as some of the best tips to keep your space clean. It might be tough to remember everything, but a lot of these tips will save you a good amount of time, so refer back to this book anytime!

Key Principles to Consider

- Identifying the root problem leading to your clutter can help you find solutions.
- Make the necessary commitment to donate, recycle, or throw away items in the house that are broken, no longer used, or no longer needed.
- Make decisions on where items belong and stick to them.

Thoughts for Reflection

- What are some of the problems you have with clutter?
- What steps can you take to solve these problems?
- What are the areas in your house that seem to attract the most clutter?

HABIT 9: CLAYGO: CLEARING VISUAL CLUTTER

Have you ever watched an episode of *Hoarders*? I remember watching it and thinking to myself that the houses were in a state of complete chaos. It takes years to reach that point. Then again, as I started sorting my own study and room, the number of items I was throwing out was alarming.

However, one thing I noticed was that the moment I cleared away the visible clutter, the room looked greatly improved already despite the chaos within the cupboards and closets I still needed to organize.

Before I dive into this, I do want to clarify one thing: Clutter is very often a symptom of hoarding, but having clutter and being a hoarder are two very different things; just because you struggle with clutter does not mean you are a hoarder. If you are a hoarder, however, it does mean there are other factors you want to deal with that extend beyond just dealing with the clutter.

Differences Between Clutter and Hoarding

Clutter and hoarding are two terms that are often used interchangeably; however, they are quite different. Clutter is just a small part of the larger problems that lead to hoarding.

However, both should be taken seriously and addressed for the sake of a person's quality of life.

Clutter is often referred to as the disorganized piles of items that can be left on the floor or other surfaces where they don't necessarily belong. Clutter can accumulate anywhere from the hallway, to the coffee table, or the kitchen counter. It might extend to your bed or chair (a universally popular place to deposit half-dirty, half-clean laundry that isn't clean enough to be put away nor dirty enough to be washed).

Clutter can be a common indication that you might be struggling with hoarding, but it by no means indicates that you have a hoarding disorder. The biggest difference between hoarding and clutter is the level of difficulty you experience when trying to get rid of items. It is not too far-fetched to say that somewhere in your house, you currently have some clutter collecting dust (don't try sneaking off and cleaning it up right now!). It could be in your closet, attic, or basement as they are common spots for clutter.

Or that kitchen counter—this is my personal weakness.

However, if you happen to find the clutter is starting to take over in other areas of your home, it can be a signal of a hoarding disorder. This means that items are starting to spill into your kitchen, bedroom, and other living spaces, filling them up with stuff to the point that going about your everyday activities is a challenge. This can be another indication of a hoarding disorder.

What Is Hoarding Exactly?

Hoarding involves the following factors:

- You are unable to get rid of items even if they carry absolutely no value.
- You find yourself getting distressed whenever things get tossed.
- You do not believe there are any other options but to keep your items.
- Certain sections of your home cannot be used because of the buildup of clutter.
- You have trouble planning and organizing events or activities in your home.

One of the common reasons hoarding occurs is the belief that every belonging you have in the house is either unique or valuable or that you might be able to use it in the future.

You might feel that the items have sentimental value. Maybe something reminds you of people you love, pets who have passed, or even just memories you are fond of. You might also get a sense of security when you are surrounded by all of your belongings, or you might be under the belief that you should not waste anything.

What Can Hoarding Do?

To start with, hoarding can directly affect your health if you are not careful. You might not think that a little extra clutter here and there could put you in danger. Large amounts of clutter can become unsanitary, increase your chances of falling, and create a fire hazard. You might also deal with feelings of isolation, anxiety, depression, and other issues.

Hoarding often causes stress as well as financial difficulties. Why? Because people who hoard often also have a shopping addiction that leads them to buying more and more unnecessary items even if they cannot afford them.

If you believe you might be struggling with hoarding, it is important that you seek professional help right away.

Dealing With Visual Clutter

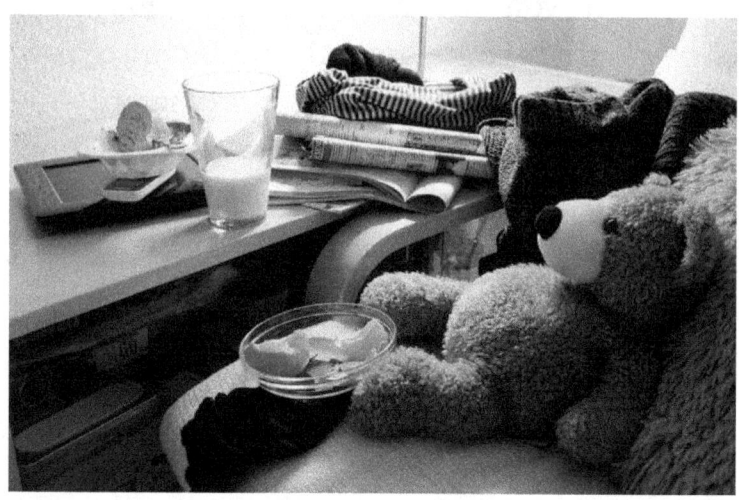

Jumping back to the task at hand, understand that visual clutter generally happens to everyone from time to time. Visible clutter is not what is stuffed in closets, attics, or under the bed but is what can be seen out in the open. The great news is that visual clutter is generally quite easy to get rid of. You just need to take a couple of steps in order to rid yourself of visible clutter.

Why exactly does visual clutter happen?

- laziness—we all have those days
- lack of communication with the people sharing the house
- overflowing drawers

- a better organizational system is needed
- taking the wrong shortcuts

For instance, you might have your entry area dedicated to your family's bags, shoes, and keys. However, if you keep getting more shoes, your entryway can become overloaded with shoes, making the area messy and stressful.

Another common area that becomes a victim of visual clutter could be your desk. Your workspace can become filled with notes and items that you think you might need; however, you tend to eventually forget to return the items to their original spaces. This can cause extra stress and distractions, so here are some strategies for clearing visual clutter:

- Focus on keeping smooth, flat areas clear. Kitchen and bathroom countertops are generally magnets for items that pile up. However, anyone wanting to get rid of clutter should focus on keeping these spaces clear. It is a common habit many people with clean homes adopt, and for someone who wants to see an end to clutter, you should consider adopting it as well. Focus on not storing items on countertops or on top of your desk.

- Clean as you go. Are you walking past that kitchen counter on the way to make yourself a cup of coffee when you notice a dish that has been left out? Take it with you to place it in the sink. Take a quick five minutes here and there to rearrange the pillows every night in the family room, encourage your kids to pick up their toys and put them back in the designated box or basket, and always try to put clean clothes away as soon as they are dry.

- Keep looking for clever DIY solutions when it comes to your storage systems. For instance, do you struggle with little items becoming clutter such as paper clips or even puzzle pieces? Have a small glass container set in the middle of the coffee table to place items like that in and put them away when you get a chance.

- Each time you use a space, spend an extra minute or two cleaning it up when you're done. It does not take that much time to keep a space neat if you're consistent about it. The problem is when you allow it to continuously accumulate clutter.

- Choose the essential items that need to be out and what can be packed away. For example, I like to keep my work and study notes with me on my desk. However, any tasks and homework that I have completed get filed away. I don't always need my art supplies out, so they can go in a box in the cupboard. Be sure to prioritize what can be kept out in the open, what should be packed away, and what should be chucked. Dealing with visual clutter is another quick way to get items that you do not need out of the house.
- Find a home for everything else. Do not revert to throwing items on the table when they don't yet have a designated place. Take your time to find a place for new items and put things right back where they belong. This is one of the best ways to avoid clutter.
- Create for yourself a set of rules and guidelines as you keep moving forward. Once you have a decluttered space, your goal is to keep it decluttered. Keep

people in the household updated about the rules of the newly decluttered spaces. Also, check in from time to time to see whether or not a space just might need to be decluttered again.

What Are the Benefits of Clearing Visual Clutter?

One benefit is that spaces without clutter are a whole lot easier to clean. You are also far less likely to build clutter in that space again as everything should hopefully have its designated place. You will feel much more at ease, will be less likely to lose things, and the house will be more functional in general. Most importantly, spending time decluttering can give you more time and energy to focus on other things that matter to you.

Clutter is always going to rear its head now and again. However, the more anti-clutter habits you adopt, the less likely you are to spot clutter. Clutter is often a consequence of a variety of bad habits, so the more focused you become on being organized, the less you will have to worry about clutter.

Depending on how well you practice your new habits, you might see an end to clutter in your home altogether. It might peek its head out once in a blue moon only to disappear just as quickly if you remain committed to your new habits, so don't give up hope when dealing with clutter. Managing clutter is more like a marathon than it is a race. It takes a great deal of time and steady effort.

Key Principles to Consider

- Clutter and hoarding are two different things. Clutter involves disorganized spaces; hoarding is a mental health problem characterized by the accumulation of items without the ability to get rid of items.
- Clear out any visual clutter first in order to improve the overall appearance of the house.
- Adopt little habits of decluttering and cleaning as you walk through the house.

Thoughts for Reflection

- What are some of your worst clutter habits?
- Do you find yourself unable to part with anything in your house?
- What steps can you take to start clearing visible clutter in your space?

HABIT 10: LABELING

One thing about spices: If they are not labeled correctly, you are bound to find a nasty surprise or two when cooking up a dish. Without clear labels, you may reach for baking powder when you really want baking soda. Sugar and salt are complete opposites, but they look very similar. Without clear containers, I always mix up salt and pepper, so I end up having a sniffing contest; if I sneeze, I know I've found the pepper.

For these reasons and more, labeling can be a very handy habit to adopt in your household, especially when you are sharing a space with other people. It can also help you find items in your home that you do not look for on a regular basis.

Labeling can be a lifesaver if done correctly.

Why Is Labeling Important?

Apart from the spice rack, naturally, what do you think labeling items can do for you? Here are some reasons why you should consider labeling everything in your home:

- It will let everyone know where things in the household should go. It might seem a tad unnecessary, but whenever more than one person shares a house, it can become chaos. Everyone has their own idea of where something should go. If everyone starts participating in chores, cleaning supplies are bound to get put in the wrong places. A good example is in the kitchen. It may be natural for you to place the spatula with the bigger utensils in the bottom drawer, but maybe your significant other prefers to place it next to the rolling pin with the pans. The thing is, without labels, things are bound to be misplaced. People may not know there is a specific place for cucumbers or that the jars go in the cupboard in the corridor and not the kitchen.

- Labeling can help to remove the visual noise. Even if you have an organized space, it can still look a little messy. If you do not know what is in your containers, you will spend a great deal of time looking for things. This is especially relevant if you bought yourself identical containers to boost the aesthetics of the house. That is all well and good; it certainly looks pretty. But be prepared to spend a good chunk of time scouring through the containers until you find the item you want. You might think you can rely on your memory, but memories are fickle when it comes to the small items in one's home. Labeling eliminates the wondering, which can be stressful, and it helps you know what's inside without having to open the container.

- Labeling allows you to make sure that everything always has a place. I have to admit that I find myself wondering where an item in the house belongs or whether it even has a designated place from time to time. Labeling can become a handy part of your organization system and make it easier to find spaces for new items or return items to their designated spaces when you are putting things away. It might take an extra few minutes while you are organizing the spaces, and although labeling is not altogether necessary, it can really make your life so much easier.
- We all know how stressful and frustrating it is to be rushing out the door and then realize you cannot find your keys. Placing labels can cut seconds and minutes off time spent looking for items in your home, especially when you suddenly want to retrieve something you have not used in a long time.
- Labeling can help to prevent clutter. When things are labeled, it makes it far easier to place the items right back where it belongs. If you are unsure about where

something needs to go and you haven't used it in the last year, chances are that you actually do not need it, and the simple solution is to just get rid of it.
- Labeling creates clarity. In a society full of distractions where everything seems to demand our attention, labeling is just one piece of calm among the chaos.

In short, labeling will save you time, increase your level of productivity, prevent a certain level of clutter, and decrease stress while inviting calm and order. It also boosts teamwork in the household when everyone finally understands where things go as it removes their excuses for why they do not place items right back where they belong.

Labeling Items in Your Home

When you organize everything, you might want to create a reminder of where everything belongs. It might not be wise to list every single item and stick it on the wall, although the idea might have crossed your mind. As the people in your home start to remember where things should go, the less the labeling will be needed.

But as you begin your home organization journey, labeling can be a very helpful tool.

But what are the specific areas in the house that will need to be labeled?

The Shared Areas

Any rooms in the house that are shared, such as the family room, laundry room, living room, garage, kitchen, exercise room, home office, and even the bathroom, should be included in your exciting labeling spree.

You'll want to label any and all shared bins and shelves in order to keep your home in general order. A label reminds you, your partner, and your kids where stuff goes. Once everyone habitually puts items in the correct place, you may consider removing the labels if you want.

Bathrooms are a very important space for labeling, primarily the linen closet. Linen closets are generally filled with a wide variety of items, and you want to group and store them in a way that is organized.

Remember to mark your toothbrushes regardless of whether they are electronic or normal. This can save you a whole lot of arguing. Everyone will simply know which toothbrush is theirs and carry on with their lives without any concern about using the wrong toothbrush.

You will also want to individually label brushes, sponges, or single-use bottles. If you recycle used bottles into cleaning products or you make homemade mixes, then labeling is not only a form of convenience, it is a necessity. Bottles containing anything other than water need to always be labeled for the sake of safety. There are plenty of products in the home that are useful but can be hazardous; even if you can keep track of unlabeled bottles, others may not be able to, so labeling is very important.

Another handy trick is to try labeling your hampers. This can help you to quickly sort the laundry. For instance, you can have one hamper labeled for light-colored clothes and another for dark clothes. This can easily save you 10 to 15 minutes of sorting each time you do the laundry.

Connected with the previous idea, you can also label individual laundry baskets to determine which is whose. This is an easy way to allow people to sort out their own laundry.

When it comes to the kitchen, you want to focus on labeling bins that fall into a specific category or group. You may want to label where spices go, as well as herbs, grains, cereal, pasta, and more.

If you happen to have a storage bin that holds extra supplies, labeling is very important as you cannot always see what is inside. Any items that come in bulk should always be labeled as well. For instance, flour and sugar look a lot alike, and if people are quick with their actions in the kitchen they can accidentally use the wrong ingredient if it is not labeled.

If you have anyone in your household who is allergic to any kind of food, then you definitely want to label those specific bins to act as a warning for people to steer clear of their allergens.

You will also want to label your craft area if you have one. The tricky thing about the craft area is the fact that you work with so many little items and tools. Keeping it organized is always tricky, even more so if you do not know what goes where. When you are working on labeling your craft supplies, make sure to separate all the items into different containers. One idea is to assign different areas for your paint supplies to keep them separate from each other. You do not want watercolor, oil, or acrylic paints to all be mixed together, right?

In your garage, you will want to label the items on the garage shelves. The garage is not usually a very popular place to hang out, and people tend to want to zip in and out when getting things. Labeling can help people find what they need quickly. Be sure to use sturdier labels as the garage can get dirty.

In your desk or office, work on keeping all your digital files organized by labeling folders and documents. You can work on labeling the physical items as well so that people who need to work in the same space or find something can do so. Labels can also help people find items that aren't theirs or that they don't often use in a pinch.

You want to label your drawers, including filing cabinet drawers. Make use of arrows and labels with the different drawers. If you have a digital filing system, then consider copying a screenshot of the files hierarchy and having it pasted into a document. You can then use arrows and write what is in each folder. You can print it out to refer back to.

Key Principles to Consider

- Labeling can help you find a place for everything.
- Labeling can help your household members find the designated places for all the items in your house.
- Labeling can save time and make life in the house more organized and efficient.

Thoughts for Reflection

- Do you have any labeled items in the house?
- How often do you find yourself looking for misplaced items in the house?
- What kind of labeling system would you like to implement in your home?

CONCLUSION

What an exciting time to end this book! Now you have a manual to guide your journey, you have the motivation, and you are ready to get going! Well, almost. Before you go, here is a quick recap of the 10 habits which were discussed in detail per chapter that you need to know to reach the peace of mind and freedom an organized, decluttered, and efficient home can bring.

You have learned why it is important to run an efficient and organized home. There are various advantages to having a clean and decluttered home including decreased stress, more time for the things you enjoy, and general peace of mind. When you have a well-organized system in place, the rest of your life will feel like it is falling into place as well. After all, a person's home is meant to be their place of refuge.

This does not mean you have to follow a stringent set of specific rules—you can use the ideas and recommendations in this book and adapt them to make a system that works for you. This means you will have to set aside a certain amount of time to figure out what you would like to accomplish, what you can realistically do, and how you can apply it in your home.

You can create for yourself a binder containing information about all the systems you have put in place. Not only does this help you keep track of everything, but anyone in the household can access and use the information to help keep the house running smoothly. You won't have to stress when dealing with things such as pets, vacations, or parties as you already have all the steps planned out. It is also incredibly handy if you find yourself away from the house and someone else has to step in to help feed pets, water plants, or otherwise take care of your home temporarily.

But won't all these new steps make everything complicated? That, again, depends on your definitions of simple and complicated. Some people thrive on stricter rules while others require more flexibility. It is entirely in your hands to decide what you want and what you do not want. All of the recommendations in this book are meant as guidelines for you to build off of, so when you are developing your system, design it in a way that makes it simple for you. You can follow looser rules or stricter rules—your choice! Your goal at the end of the day is to make your life easier and give you freedom from the stress of maintaining your home.

With that, you have also learned how to deal with procrastination and have learned about the one-minute rule. The one-minute rule says that if you come across a task that will take you less than one minute to do, then you should deal with it straight away. This can prevent many procrastination issues in the future.

Along with that, you want to get into the habit of putting things back where they belong right away. In order to adopt this habit, you will first need to designate a place for everything.

Once you have done that, you can employ various clever storage tactics in different areas of the house in order to reduce clutter. Even so, remember that clutter is not always avoidable.

Remember to try and identify the reasons you are allowing clutter to accumulate and work out a viable solution. When it comes to matters of clutter, it is recommended to hold a family meeting to disseminate information on how things will be working in the future as you want to deal with clutter as a family. Once you are in the habit of dealing with clutter, including visual clutter, you will immediately be seeing a huge difference in the efficiency of your house.

Have patience with yourself as implementing an entirely new system can take time. You are going to have your ups and downs while working on forming new habits and breaking bad ones. It is a very exciting journey, so allow yourself to have fun while doing it!

If you share a household with roommates or family, you'll want to get them on board with this journey as well. It might take some time to convince them, or it might not be a struggle at all. Regardless, when sharing a house, the burden of keeping it running efficiently should not fall on the shoulders of one individual alone.

So although this book is complete, your journey to the freedom of an organized, decluttered, and efficient home is just beginning. Remember to revisit the tips and strategies shared in this book every now and then to help with motivation and to keep you moving forward. Keeping an organized and efficient home is not easy, but the rewards that come with it are well worth the time and effort. You will find that many other aspects of your life are going to flourish because it all comes back to how you feel in your home. Your home is meant to be your safe space which is what this book is all about: Creating a peaceful, calming place to rest your head.

CPSIA information can be obtained
at www.ICGtesting.com
Printed in the USA
BVHW051600280423
663230BV00011B/124